Stoma in a teacup

Neil Raffan

Copyright © 2024 Neil Raffan

All rights reserved.

ISBN: 979-8-8791-1700-4

For Karen, Kevin, Louise, Paul, Sue and
Tony … and all who saw me through

Thank you - x

Doreen Grimshaw
24/6/37 – 19/6/24

In the beginning

Hello!

This is a patient's take on *This is going to hurt*.

This is my take.

I am Neil Raffan Andrews. I was born on the island of Mauritius on the fourteenth of June in 1954.

So?

Exactly. Part of me couldn't agree more.

Except …

Arthrogryposis Multiplex Congenita (AMC) is the name of my condition, with resultant disability. By all means Google it before you proceed. And if it registers then you are already many steps ahead of most of the medical profession that I have had to deal with during the timeframe of this diatribe. Whilst I accept that AMC is a rare condition this is not an acceptable excuse for not reading the patient's notes. It is not like checking you can still state your full name and date of birth; the ad infinitum of those two questions I do understand, in context. But the *I don't really care but is it arthritis* IS NOT ACCEPTABLE.

Dear reader, for your information, AMC has no uniform template for how it affects those so born, and I have always considered myself lucky in that awful sense of there always being someone worse off.

Within these pages my review of the NHS is very far from positive. Whilst I hundred percent agree that it is hugely under-funded it is as equally mismanaged.

Though my private sector experience was more limited the same premise applies, that it is the excellent staff that keep the health service afloat with above the call of duty care. I know how ill I have been and how their gentleness has seeped into me during crises, helping me make my way through to and up the gradient to the healthier side of life. A soft touch or word after a somewhat harsher exchange from those that should not be in the healthcare business; those that refuse to wipe bottoms, those than refuse to answer call buttons. Other than earning a living what are you doing in the profession?

Patience with patients, however trying we may be – if you don't have it, please leave. This is not the place but my experience of care homes features similar staffing issues, the angels and the over brusque. There should be no place in end-of-life care for such harshness, however challenging one's brain's vagaries make one's behaviour. Where the person I visited was allowed to be abused solely because she did not react to said abuse. Is being tugged at and incessantly followed by another demented soul not abuse. There were plenty staff, happy to sit idly with the *still* inmates, all blankly staring at the drone of daytime television. Staff indolence is harsh on the patients. This same home had expelled another friend's husband for violent behaviour! I wonder?

For another time, another place …

I truly do appreciate how lucky I am, and also how annoying I am to think so, and this tale in no way is meant to belittle what others have and are going through with having a stoma suddenly thrust itself into the part and parcel of their lives.

Respect.

Glossary

AMC – arthrogryposis multiplex congenita
ASU – Ambulatory Surgical Unit
DILF – Dad's I'd like to fuck
GTCS – General Teaching Council for Scotland
IBS – irritable bowel syndrome
Moke - *read* woke
Obs – temperature, blood pressure and level of oxygen in the blood
PrEP – Pre-Exposure Prophylaxis
PRUH – Princess Royal University Hospital
RADAR key – Royal Association for Disability and Rehabilitation key
RHS – Royal Horticultural Society

SA&A Unit/ SA&AU – Ambulatory Surgical Unit … I know, go figure!

UVF – Ulster Volunteer Force

October 4th, 2021

Immediately before the fourth becomes the fifth, and then again, immediately after I was connected to Paul.

Both calls before the morphine, I had chosen to live.

Fairytale

I am gay. Tick! I am disabled. Tick! But are two ticks really enough nowadays?

I am not a one-legged, black, lesbian nun. If only.

Nor am I a lesbian, with one-leg, who happens to be both black and a nun.

Not even a nun who has one leg, and is a black lesbian …

You get the picture. I have two ticks but I am not

woke. In fact, if truth be told, and it shall, I was convinced it was *moke* as opposed to woke, that's how unwoke I am.

But I have two ticks and a stoma.

Any points for the stoma, for being single, for having a cat? Or even, in modern parlance, for being an old fart?

*

And, I idly wonder what the title of my oeuvre would be in French? Such moments of distraction, or madness, as I recall my friend, and former colleague, Enfer-Poulet, and wonder what she would suggest *Stoma in a Teacup* should retail as in France … *Une tempête dans un verre d'eau*? actually *Une stomie dans un verre d'eau*, though I feel sure she would come-up with a pithier title but, moving on, somewhat quickly …

*

How much background is needed? What do you need to know to put all this in context? Will your context be the stoma or AMC or both? Choices.

*

Back in the day there was no choice for my parents, my mother. And I know this freaks out my elder brother, but if my mother had had a choice would she have taken it. You cannot be subjective over abortion because you have to realise that this isn't about the you that you now are but relates to the you that preceded you being.

I continue to be amazed by the fact that in our current century parents are still struggling to receive the right AMC diagnosis for their children. Yet, should I be, aren't my own experiences proof enough. I can count on the bent fingers of one hand how often a medical practitioner has recognised my condition as opposed to having to ask me to literally spell it out. Even I usually lose an r or misplace one in arthrogryposis, when the profession asks me to spell the word.

Whenever I attend our support group's family weekends, I believe I have two valuable points to share with parents of children. Do not forget the disabled child's siblings, parental love and care needs to be distributed equitably and visibly for one; and, do not deny the disability, be consistent in your approach. The first point may appear obvious but it is not so easy to put into practice, especially if your AMC child requires more than its fair share of care. The reality of the disability issue is so important for expectation, both the child's and that of the parents. This said, nowadays, the sky does indeed seem the limit with equal opportunities defying gravity. But dear parents, please ensure that they don't defy reality.

I was born on a little speck in the Indian Ocean, which though my parents dragged me to and from Great Ormond Street in 1956, was retrospectively a safe harbour for my first thirteen years of living as a child with AMC. Whilst I do fully understand when adults finally confront the abuse that occurred to them as children, resurrecting it from what, twenty or thirty years previously for my part I struggle to recollect what follows. As part of my vocal precocity, combined with single status and innate nature, I collected my parents' friends as my own friends. One of which, who had been a neighbour in Mauritius, advised quite some time after both my parents had died, that she used to feel for me as she heard my screams as my mother attempted to drag me off to physiotherapy for my hands. I have absolutely ZERO recall of this, to this day … this day will soon see me reach seventy! What I do recall is my mother vocalising her frustration with my fingers when I struggled to tie my shoelaces, blaming me for their lack of dexterity as my beseeching had won the day and she had stopped the finger physiotherapy. Interesting. I know how I would have handled me, even back then, also interesting that my mother, a primary school teacher by training, gave up on her son. Though in the midst of her retrospective I was to learn of the ongoing issues within the marriage that she was also dealing with. So, for the sake of expediency and a quieter life, she chose an immediate solution that resulted in long term damage. I make that statement as a fact not to attach blame; on two counts, I know I was willful, even with no recall of the pre-physio meltdowns, secondly my mother made so many right decisions with regards to my initial care … again appreciated retrospectively. Top of the list being following the orthopaedic surgeon's advice that my hands should not be operated on, thus the scream-the-house-down visits to the physiotherapist. The treatment of AMC by the medical profession seems to me to have followed fads, operate, splints, both … plus extensive physio. The generation that followed me appear to be those that had their hands operated on. Yes, giving them open palms, but fixed, so no finger dexterity. They have had to adapt, and AMCs do adapt. From my take though, however off putting my proffering of a bunched-up fist as a handshake is my life is adapted? Is adapted the correct word for me? I believe it is for those with AMC who have had an operation giving them Edward Scissorhands' hands, but my hands have not. Yes, my feet have adapted their gait to their respective post-op selves. Preserve appears as the closest word that is opposite to adapt. With perseverance replacing adaption; though that would indicate a struggle, whereas the actual bottom-line struggle is learning. Learning to adapt means unlearning a previous practice. Take holding a pencil, for example, I didn't, contrary to common parlance adapt my hands so as to be able to write. I have always held a pencil that way.

The operations on both pre-school feet were in order to flatten my upward curving soles, removing my involuntary *stationary* rocking motion!

I have previously mentioned adaption, how apt

with regards to life post-stoma, but generally not to life with AMC. Why? Well I have known nothing different to the AMC affected limbs, the operations on both feet taking place before I was three years old. Whilst the need of the 6th of October ileostomy may have been building up since birth it was not visible and from my teens onwards mis-diagnosed.

Adaption is one of the things that was always so there at the front of my mind with regards to having children, and teaching them. Take my experience with my friends' children. I have always had to take a step back when showing them how to do something, for children will want to copy my fingers, as they are learning, and it is futile for me to say *hold it properly* when they are being good little pupils and doing as I am. Perhaps if you are left-handed or have a left-handed child or sibling this will be easier to understand or appreciate.

As to whether bed-wetting into my teens was AMC related, I do not know. What I do now know is that the gut issues that started in my teens, and were misdiagnosed for decades, were related to AMC.

And what about the even bigger elephant in my room, yes even bigger than disability, homosexuality. Yes, even pre-school ... I believe ... or it's what I remember ... what I recall beyond and above any physio trauma ... is playing with dolls, and there is even a perverse foggy sense of wearing girls' clothes ... an under-five drag queen. Really? I know there was a general protect policy, that I was not strong enough for the rough and tumble of boys' play. But! But who would have sanctioned dressing me as a girl. And how did that fit in with the uber religious beliefs that both parents appeared to have held.

Back to actual homosexuality, and I do not feel like using the term gay because of that word's joyful connotation for this is not a particularly happy recall. If I was to lie on the proverbial couch and unburden myself, I would say that my first sexual arousal (that I recall) occurred when I was around six years old. But in the somewhat bizarre situation of being on holiday with my parents at, at the time, Mauritius's only holiday hotel. Le Chaland was built for the various military personnel that were based on the island. Which, during the sixties up to independence, meant the navy. Civilians were allowed to holiday at Le Chaland if occupancy was not taken up by the armed forces.

That particular evening, I was locked in my mother's bedroom and my younger brother was locked in my father's, presumably for our safety, at bedtime. What I remember is waking and crying my eyes out at the door imagining that this Dutch man with a goatee was coming for me. Pure imagination and perverse longing. A six-year-old with a man-hair kink? This fetish with facial and body hair was something I could not deny to my teenage self once puberty eventually struck. But it was late. Annoying really, as I myself have always been punctiliously punctual. I was body hairless way too long and used to yearn for my father's chest of hair. Walks up and down Union Street in Aberdeen hoping to spy tufts at the tops of T-shirts or better still open-necked shirts. The envy of sexually developed twelve-year-olds with forested armpits, or classmates who shaved daily, sported popstar length sideburns, or classmates in the art's club who already had chest hair. When would I need my first shave?

I first kissed a girl in Mauritius, the same one who informed me indirectly that Father Christmas was in fact my parents by advising me that I was receiving the watch I had requested within my *Dear Santa* letter – two traumas instigated by the one eight-year-old. Such scarring!

My poor mother ended up giving me my official sex education, though by then my class mate Graham Smart had introduced me to *The Naked Ape*. Poor Graham was neither homosexual nor smart; he was lippier than my good self but with no appropriate off button when heading dangerously out beyond his depth, both with teachers and peers. His precarious tenure of places in local schools ended with his aged parents signing him up to a cadet branch of the military. So, I put my mother through the trial of telling me about the birds and the bees. I remember forcing the issue, interestingly enough whilst I was in her single bed having wet myself in mine, oh yes … I was still bed wetting as my sixteenth birthday approached. This latter fact being part of the reason an incontinent bottom, post stoma reversal, seemed a bit of a *comeback to bite me* issue from my childhood. To bite me on my arse no less. The joys, dear reader, that await you within.

I would say that I was still emotionally a child

whilst being instructed that sexual intercourse was the culmination of love.

Though I searched out the hirsute of my age I did not yet have queer in my vocabulary. Did my siblings spot it? My younger had called me out once as a teenager, solely on his own embarrassment when we collided as he exited the bathroom naked; whilst the elder stated he had always known when I finally came out. Did my father? That remained undisclosed during his remaining lifetime, whilst for my mother, dealing with the physical reality of me appeared to allow her to place any non-masculine behaviour at the door of AMC. This said, an attempt in 1980 to disclose my sexuality failed as homosexuality was allegedly a treatable condition … recanting was wrong, but way easier than accepting the need of treatment.

At the time, the bottling it all up reinforced through hypothetical discussions with a close female friend who viewed homosexuality as abnormal. Whilst refuting abnormal I conceded unnatural. This to a good Catholic girl who saw no contradiction in heterosexual promiscuity.

Not wanting to be homosexual an unhealthy

option to do battle with. Oh! the futility of the struggle against my reality for all those years.

My parents' generation, despite living through the second of the World Wars, was one that still knew its place in Britain's class riddled society. And the medical profession was up there, if you recall the satirical skit of who looks up to who? I had refused the physiotherapy option, sobeit, my choice. My choice as a toddler? Okay a screaming one. But *my* choice! Really?

Moving on, and we were now living in the tropical island of Aberdeen, and the focus was on my education and university entrance. The catch-up required was huge, the pace in Mauritius was in such a low gear that I had a lot of ground to make up. An awful lot. So much so that I was exempt from *games*, so as to enable, particularly my maths, to achieve the necessary grades. Allegedly with the assistance of my mother but definitely not with the assistance of my teacher. Mr Malloch was in dispute with the General Teaching Council for Scotland, I believe he refused to sign-up to the recently established GTCS and the city council suspended and subsequently sacked him. He was not the only one to suffer, his maths classes were no longer devoted to maths but to his putting the rights of a man to us thirteen in Maths 7, the dunces and misfits. Looking back, I realise that I was not the only homosexual in that class but not at the time. At the time fellow pupil Andrew was just creepy, strange.

Looking back, so, so easy to do. Who is there to stop me? To contradict the view? One of the biggest parental mistakes, okay my mother's, was absolving me from games. Hypothetical, I know, but I do feel it could have either helped with my physical acceptance by my peers or with my would-be-nascent sexuality. Perhaps both? But no. It was not to be and I struggled with both. Though interestingly, once the O level results were announced, I was accepted as something other than a freak by three of the four brightest boys, who were also the three of the top athletes. I had generally been placed in lower class groups than my innate ability as befitting someone coming from the backward colonies combined with the widely held view that physical and mental disability went hand-in-hand. I recall my mother's battles on her insistence that I was not special needs fodder and could stand on my own two feet in a normal co-ed school. The fourth of my year's brainboxes was not at all sporty but sadly he was far too serious at being intelligent than my flippant self ever could be. So, I was stuck to the *excused games* club of asthmatic and fat. *Moke is moi!*

And anyway, I was one of the school's two spastics according to the new deputy head. I kid you not. *So, you are the other spastic*, pronounced Patricia Cormack, on my first encounter with her. I am afraid I hated her from then on. Her take on education at the start of the 1970's was not one of assimilation, no, her view was that the spastics, the thalidomide girl and the AMC boy, should be at special schools, not mixing with the physically pure pupils of her school. Those were the days.

Yes, those last four words have a flippant edge but they also show that I survived however painful the process. My new popularity, through both exam results and throwing myself into the drama club, as well as being a goody-two-shoes from the majority of my teachers' perspective had put me on the list of possible prefects. I am certain as I can be without proof that Patricia Cormack put the kybosh on that happening.

Amazing that she didn't stop me dancing in front

of the Queen! Though I am sure she must have tried. I can but imagine the exchange, the three drama teachers were made of stern stuff. Yes, the Queen *opened* our new school building; and yes too, I may be exaggerating the size of the thorn she perceived me to be.

Another memory that my brain buried so deeply that I cannot recall it but through my mother's retelling is of my first day of school in Mauritius. Allegedly I bawled my eyes out, sitting on the veranda, refusing to re-enter the classroom where the *normal* children had laughed at me. Precocious or what, *how can Jesus love me* I asked? It would appear that religion and I were bound to fall out from the start. I did end up enjoying school, all my schools when compared to my university experience, thanks mainly to the better teachers who inspired me to believe and achieve and made it enjoyable.

I don't think the inherent selfishness of the university staff is solely to blame for me finding it all a somewhat antiseptic experience. Thankfully my delayed puberty made for no embarrassing school crushes. I may have found certain senior boys or even classmates physically attractive, but to my mind that seemed like a yearning to

Stoma in a teacup

look like them rather than have sex with them.

Sex! What did sex actually entail? From my understanding Desmond Morris had described the mechanics. Love-sex/Sex-love. So very confusing. At university I was at my most muddled and unhappy sexually. Many of my fellow attendees, like me, went to their home town university. For six months or so of my first year I had dated the school dux; she was far too intelligent for me. I knew but didn't know. Was it because of the AMC? The joy and relief if it were down to being disabled that made me asexual. And I was asexual, wasn't I? The thoughts I had of men were merely a physical wish fulfilment yearning regarding myself... weren't they? The he-man I wanted to be. Or? I wished that I had the gumption to become the first AMC Ziggy Stardust whilst all the while stopping myself from becoming *a lad insane*. Oh Mr Bowie ... and even retrospectively I lie, for my mother had inculcated physical normalcy within my psyche that AMC didn't really figure at this particular juncture, it was more a question of what was my sexual orientation. In retrospection, even that is too grandiose for there was but the one direction, the problem was that I had no propulsion to move in it. With regards to peers there was one fellow

23

student who appeared like an off-set Top of the Pops glam rock ingenue; a stand-out campus celebrity, but not in a positive role model sense, more in a finger pointing one. But, how deep do I drill, is that my take as opposed to that of the student body as a whole. Yes, I can admit that he scared me a bit, the thought that that could be me. Was it me? My future?

My closest school/university friend *had* to marry his long-term girlfriend and drop out of university to support the burgeoning family. For my next trick I disguised, hid, lied, take your pick all apply with regards to my homosexual self in the company of an on the spectrum (in today's parlance) straight man and a woman who had a degenerative physical condition. Safety assumed. What could go wrong? My sanity was so laden with other layers of stuff.

Financial buoyancy was another family dictum that I chose not to be able to shake off throughout my life. My mother told me that she had returned to work in 1970 so as to keep my father in the lifestyle to which he had become accustomed in Mauritius. This was the point from which my mother started divulging her marital confidences, unhappiness. And whilst my father may have claimed the tax credit for my time at university it was my mother who *topped up* my paltry grant with an equally paltry amount; and I was not allowed a part-time job because of my innate physical weakness. Normal one minute, disabled the next – the parents' right to choose. The child's right to take cover? Which was taken in my bedroom, within the shallow world of pop music. I chose to spend my disposable income on vinyl, most generally, and not at the students' union. Again, perhaps my own poignant mixture of reasons, my voice was never one that worked within a noisy hubbub. As I inexorably approach seventy years of age, I appreciate that my voice has been a lifelong let down. Did I ruin my vocal cords with all that screaming when being dragged off to physio as a toddler? I jest. I believe the fact that my voice does not penetrate others eardrums is due to a combination of the pitch and my breathing capacity. A challenge heightened by the management positions I ended up in, as well as during my tenure as a tennis club chairman. Though my capacity to stand upright unaided was obviously much better than now it was even then not my chosen stance. Totally against my mother's wishes I had done part of a midsummer charity walk; I managed eighteen miles. My mother blamed this for my now chronic toe issues. The walk cannot have helped but I believe that at last I had had my hormonal growth spurt and the AMC body was out of kilter. At this time, I started to realise that as one aged, left childhood, that the medical profession was less and less interested in AMC other than in the sense of an occasional box ticked should the condition come anywhere near its remit. It was at university that I started to be shod in surgical footwear. Though there was no alternative if I wanted to stay on my feet these surgical shoes and subsequent boots affected my view of myself as a desirable catch. How I hated catching my reflection in shop windows, who is that clod-clopping along in footwear fit for Lurch from the Addams Family? For my elder brother's wedding I bought a pair of maroon platform heels and lasted in them until the meal. The agony of fashion. Twat! I couldn't be what I wasn't. But what was I?

Can I use cigarette smoke as an excuse for the dysfunctional vocal cords, was it a factor as I was brought up in a household where both parents were heavy if not quite chain smokers, followed by a working environment with surround-air as opposed to sound of cigarettes? Passive is Nels!

My now married school friend had been the sole friend as much into pop music as myself, there was now no-one to share that side of my life. I did go to football, with our neighbour's oldest offspring. He was three years my junior and my recall is that I was, if anything, interested in the manliness of a couple of the first team players as opposed to him. The question of his own sexuality was only to register on my radar on the couple of occasions when he visited me in London. And my *spectrum* university friend followed me to London. I had done my usual, applied for a civil service post and been successful, without thinking beyond what it meant ... in any shape or form. I do wonder if my mother actually realised that this would mean that I would be leaving home, ending up five hundred or so miles away. The Crown Agents for Oversea Governments and Administrations would be my employer.

Who would have thought? Did I? I don't think so, not even subliminally. Previous to the actual flight from Aberdeen, actually an overnight train, I had wondered if anyone I shared a sleeper compartment with on my various journeys south for failed interviews with commercial firms would have tried anything on. I cannot now recall any lust buckets but something must have triggered the imagination to ponder on such things. Having been so tardy at kicking the bed wetting habit wet dreams were in one sense an unwelcome reminder of incontinence.

Now, I can see, that I spent the first three years in London in a schizophrenic dilemma. Twist or stick? Stay or return? The allure of my only gay role model's lifestyle versus the safety of home. Tart versus eunuch.

All a massive exaggeration, in one sense, in another all consuming. I knew it was unhealthy but. And how the buts built up, as I was literally walking out of my built-up shoes. A lad insane remembers losing his right shoe in the scrum at Earl's Court tube station after seeing the had-been Thin White Duke.

Bunny, said role model, was the welcoming party that almost pre-dawn Saturday morning. If my mother had only known. Talk about entering the lion's den; though the queen's parlour more like. An eye opener? Not 'arf! A veritable jaw dropper. *Well, hello! Who have we queer, I mean here?* my introduction or his introduction? Does it matter, darling!

Yes, Bunny is camp. At the time he seemed all too outrageous, even within the confines of our civil service accommodation. Simon was, in appearance straighter laced than myself, whilst Duncan (a fellow Scot) was as promiscuous a rabbit as Bunny – but straight. Yes, I was picking up on the terms if still not wearing mine quite on my sleeve as Bunny. He had lodged the longest in the annex to our employer's hostel and was monthly reminded that his tenure was up. *Who'll pay for this rent on the streets?* he would screech upon receipt of the official letters. Allegedly we had six months to find our feet. Simon and I had already agreed to flat share, *the invisibles* as both Bunny and Duncan affectionately called us, the antithesis of the troublesome twosome. True, Simon and I did willingly give the floor to Duncan and Bunny. Less the conversation, less the exposure. And as at the time neither Simon nor I were that verbose it suited, there was never a need to flex testosterone muscles that neither possessed. Should, at any time, conversation of a personal nature surface then in Simon's case it would be about books and his current reading matter, whilst my sharing always seemed to revolve around pop music. He would always return from Hatchards with a new purchase and

I was similarly self-indulgent with visits to Our Price Records.

Bunny was no role model for me to follow, said who? Me. But I did, as surreptitiously as I could. Initially within our four. Beefcake Duncan seemed to relish the excursions to the gay bars the most, The Salisbury or The Queen's Head, revelling in the gawps whilst Bunny twirled, with Simon and I skulking behind the pair. Simon was emotionally shy whilst in my case it was my physicality … all too exposed in the presence of beauty. The skip over, embarrassed looks reminded me of the ones I saw myself give any unexpected mirror reflection. This was all even more of a beauty pageant than the boy-girl world. One-on-one facially there was not much to choose, I would say, between the four flatmates; but, though poles apart, Duncan and Bunny had physical presences that neither Simon nor I possessed, he shrunk within his frame whilst I tried to pose as least disabled as possible, only gripping my vodka and tonic when I thought no-one was looking. Yet, oh yes, yet I went back for more … initially with but Bunny, then on my own. My actual behaviour never changed. And after a couple of times being ripped-off I realised that this was not my milieu.

Stoma in a teacup

Shifting location to The King's Head in Poland Street made no difference, I confounded my offense of being disabled by arriving (and leaving) too early and sitting in a corner reading a book (usually one of Simon's recommended but impenetrable thick tomes). Did my silent curses aimed at Huxley, Sterne or Hesse transmit across the pub floor. I tried to hide my legs below the table and look as un-disabled as possible. I was in the bears' den … hirsute heaven. Suddenly I was no longer the follicle free youth but developing my own full, abundant even, chest of hair and could now actually grow a full beard. I couldn't bulk up though, did this rule me out from even being a cub? So many rules and regs even in this world.

Perhaps not a minefield but traipsing a path though the world of the homosexual was not as straightforward as man meets man. Tops/bottoms, bears/cubs, masters/slaves … the permutations went on and on.

One Saturday night, a couple of years after our dispersal from our original flat-share Bunny caught me in The King's Head. I didn't come out to Bunny, obviously he always knew, but he had never spelt it out to me, not even whilst disclosing that he had the hots for Simon. Though I always teased Bunny that it was Simon's bulge he had the hots for since bursting into our room early on one Shrove Tuesday morning in a tizz about his pancake batter.

When we ever recalled those days, he claimed that he was using his alleged lust for Simon as an opening for me to escape from my confines. And oh boy, or should that be oh man? Anyway, did he give me some lecture that night in The King's Head about my do-not-disturb book reading body posture? Pow! There, I was out … well to two people. Bunny and Steven. I could see why Steven was at The King's Head the archetypal gay bear a gentle, stocky, bearded fellow. Was Bunny his cub? Though I could in those days converse in the codified, but less expansive vocabulary of the current gay lexicon, was I really *out*.

Having Bunny and Steven know was, for sure, an extremely healthy safety valve, but? I was not out. Did it matter? Was I still denying my sexuality at twenty-five? Was I as much of a eunuch as Bunny was wont to label Simon? When Simon, who had switched to the Foreign

Office, received his first overseas posting I bit the solitary confinement bullet within SE19. My parents assisted all three sons with their first step on the property ladder. An address as confused as me – a London postcode within the outer borough of Croydon. What to make of us both?

But being out to Bunny was actually the beginning of the end of our closeness and subsequently our friendship. Being out to him was not enough, the fact that I was not out to all and sundry meant more to him than our friendship. Or looked at from his perspective our friendship wasn't enough of a backbone support for me to feel able to face the world as a homosexual man. I wasn't Bunny. I was me. And me had always stated to himself that he needed a partner by his side before telling the world, that is my mother. How else would I be able to survive the misdiagnosis of my homosexuality as being a mental illness. And to think how she had battled to ensure I attend mainstream schooling. Flippancy by way of reducing the swearing ...

All this surface veneer without appreciating the inner turmoil, literally, of my guts. Despite my claims to be an empty husk I had inner turmoil that would prove impossible to diagnose.

Neither Simon nor I had ever brought anyone home. Our homes remained where our respective parents lived. I assumed he was as much the monk I hated being. However, sex did occur at least once in our flat share. Simon missed it! He had gone travelling in the south of France for a couple of weeks, so his younger brother and his girlfriend came up to London for the middle weekend, the flat wasn't soundproof. I didn't say anything, neither to Piers nor to Simon upon his return. It would have seemed, would have been, prudish.

Mum remained the word as the London Borough of Croydon welcomed its latest disabled homosexual virgin. It didn't need declaring on the mortgage documents and the life insurance policy form had yet to cater for the AIDS generation, blood tests and the DENIED stamp. I can't even claim to have slipped under the radar prior to or even in that brief *catch your breath* moment of Rock Hudson's death.

Over the decades of years, I have learnt how to detach my physicality from my sexual identity. But the total fantasy of doing so lasts a brevity that depends on factors such as is the object of lust in my life or not, or but on the periphery of it, or basically an out of reach pop or film star? The latter work best with the non-disabled me, though we still switch the lights off. Of course, I'm being flippant. Give me a break. And Rock Hudson had died, long live Doris Day.

So, as I couldn't really walk in my shoes my right ankle was fused and the orthopaedic surgeon at Westminster Hospital prescribed surgical boots as the way to go forward. He also prescribed operating on the left foot until the morning of the operation. I had been prepped, nil by mouth, shaved lower shin … and lo and behold the surgeon appears and asks, somewhat aggressively, who recommended this operation? 'You did,' didn't really go down that well with him, his hangers-on managed not to smirk. Words like unnecessary and pointless drifted into fade as he stomped off and I was left on the cliff edge of anticipation. Work was not expecting me back for at least three months, my parents were reconciled to having me home for most of that time, the Gardners, my landing neighbours, had my spare key …

Yes, there was psychological trauma. No-one

could believe it. Least of all me. The way the orthopaedic surgeon walked away as if it was my fault, as if I was the con artist in this farce of his own creation. Had he been sleepwalking when authorising the letters advising me of the left leg operation. Forty or so years on I would no doubt be advised to litigate. Thank goodness it was back then, forty years on there would be enough health issues going on.

I cannot recall having stomach cramps during my childhood in Mauritius. The first recollection of their occurrence is in Aberdeen, and randomly at that. Like my father I had both a big appetite and a fast metabolism, but unlike my father but unbeknownst to me (or I believe my parents) it was not solely my limbs that had been affected by AMC. The placement within my body of my internal organs did not replicate that of a normal person. I traipsed through life blithely ignorant of this additional blessing.

So, Neil was as physically perfect as the orthopaedic world could make, time to get out there and mingle. Right? If only Neil had had such bare faced cheek. I readily admit the cheek was there, but it was never bare faced in the homosexual world, the gay world, the bear world.

And pre-phone lines, pre-internet there was the Lonely Heart columns of the likes of Time Out as well as some of the newspapers, eventually including the local freebie. Other than the pubs, other than the cottages. To think, when I left Scotland the 1967 Act of Parliament that covered England and Wales had yet to apply to north of the border ... let alone to Northern Ireland. Crazy! But fact, and perhaps, just perhaps, added to my university myopia.

Thank goodness for friends, albeit straight, but then so was I, who kept me afloat as I dealt with the status quo me, as opposed to the me that was anticipating having a more normal gait. This was as good as it was going to gait! (Flippancy rules.) One thing to be said for the surgical boots was that they didn't slip off at inopportune moments like the surgical shoes were prone to do as it did not take long for my walk to disable them, flattening out the heels. There was still pain, always pain. Even with made-to-measure boots it would seem that I continued to walk with the pressure firmly on my two big toes. So along with surgical boots I now also had regular podiatry. The aim of the latter was to keep me on my feet and attempt to avoid ulceration on the base pressure points. A lot depended on the frequency of the podiatry visits. Hark at me, podiatry, back in the Eighties it was called chiropody! But hey, if they want to aggrandise it to podiatry so be it, as long as I benefit and can walk pain free. That was not going to happen but I generally felt the benefit from each visit. My work colleagues always enjoyed smirking at the thought of me having my balls rubbed. Balls of my feet. All good, unless they had accidentally taken off too much hard skin and punctured the exposed surface skin ... it happened far too regularly. I actually reported one podiatrist, less than ten years ago, who caused me to bleed on three successive visits ... solely by being slap dash sloppy. Her superior asked me if I wanted to make an official complaint, but I told Maria (who had been my NHS podiatrist for a couple of years before her promotion) that my intent was solely for her information purposes and to assist her in pre-empting a particular problem. I used to be in management, my glib stock phrase whenever I gave gratuitous advice. Though, obviously, I didn't vocalise my thoughts, to that extent on the telephone call to Maria.

Back to as good as it's going to get and time to mingle ... whilst still within his orbit Bunny suggested I try my luck with Time Out. What had

I got to lose? I could step away at each phase, this was me replying to others' adverts as opposed to posting my own. Though a total lack of replies to my own responses was slightly unnerving I, again under Bunny's tutelage, placed my own advert. Would I find my *bear*, was I anyone's idea of a *cub*? Was I anyone's idea? Let's see. Don't over think it all Neil. No, Bunny was doing that for me.

How to cut this story short without diminishing it? This story is but another phase. Most of it tragic, and by most, I mean ninety-nine percent. With Time Out correspondence, prior to emails and texting, there was further letter writing or landline telephone calling, if either party was willing to share that level of personal information. And, eventually the meet-up ... or should that be the stood-up. What a twat I used to be. I would actually wait for two hours for the no-show not to show. Two hours! Seems ridiculous from this distance and at this age, but then I was an ever-hopeful mug, a belief in my age and obviously a complete denial in my visual physical self, that's the trouble with avoiding the reflection. I didn't see what they saw, and I couldn't really blame them, would I have dated someone in a wheelchair or blind? Good question, and the truthful answer is not, definitely not if I had gone on the date without the for knowledge of the date's physical state.

My crux? Twist or stick? Tell or shush? I tried to convince myself that my personality would win them over ... but those who left me at street corners, on park benches or by post boxes saw the physicality, and that was enough. That's if they ever showed at all. The height of my humiliation was crying down the phone whilst calling one of the Time Out no-show punters from a red phone box; where are you? He didn't pick up after my first call had him dumbfounded at my not understanding the rules. Had I no shame, as I continued in my attempts to reach him? Leonard had known about my disability. Therefore, had it been its actual reality, or my face, had he even turned up. In his case I felt he had clocked me, for from where I stood waiting outside The Swan, I was convinced that the someone I thought might be Leonard had spied me.

Sad but true etc. And there was Malcolm. Malcolm who freed me of my virginity if not my cherry, so to speak. It was the Notting Hill Carnival weekend, a fun weekend all round. He was a sweet and considerate teddy-bear of a bloke, about ten years older than my good self and much more worldly in what I later learnt was a gay queen sense that I could never quite muster up to or master for that matter ... you know; the opera, the fine wine, the de rigueur reading material. Malcolm had not heard of The Boomtown Rats! I felt sure that come 1984 and Band Aid he would have, courtesy of Sir Bob. Though he was unlikely to ever source my random lyric of the day, *it's a tonic for the troops*[1]. And my Time Out success and failure ratio did not alter with the advent of Malcolm, who thankfully was not a come and go one off. He was genuine, in the sense of sensibility, and gentle in his exploration of the physical body I inhabited. The affair may have lasted beyond the year's end if my inclination had matched his availability, and status. As one of Auntie's foreign correspondents he was regularly assigned work that took him overseas. Malcolm was of South African origin, though that had nothing to do with the fact that I accidentally found out that I was a fling. I nearly typed BUT a fling, that would however be disingenuous, as he always made me feel that I was his sole attention

---

[1] She's so modern – Bob Geldof, J. Fingers, Kevin Sharkey.

when in his company and was also very sweetly amused by my lack of knowledge let alone appreciation for the classics; not just opera, but also mythology alongside Tolstoy and Molière. Could I differentiate the Dutch from the Flemish masters, tell a Tintoretto from a Caravaggio? Who, what, where, when? I was in awe and enjoyed the sex with benefits. The opening of my eyes and ears as well as ...

But one day someone other than Malcolm answered his landline whilst he was, unbeknownst to me, away on assignment. Until then he had been meticulous in filling my own diary with his times away. It was probably a last-minute thing, and I had slipped his mind. As I found out, understandably. I didn't blurt out *who are you?* but amazingly kept my cool, merely stating my name when asked who was calling after being informed Malcolm was away until Saturday week.

A letter with a first-class stamp was on my doormat before I even attempted another telephone call. I wish I had kept it, for I don't want to bad mouth him forty plus years later. He told me about Clem, and how their respective on-the-road jobs allowed for an open relationship and basically that though he could easily continue with us being friends with benefits that he did not wish to either lead me on, or hurt me anymore than finding out about Clem may have done already. Whilst I had enjoyed the fling, and all his attention, I did not want to be knowingly but someone's latest fuck buddy.

One of the things that I missed most with the end of the affair was Malcolm's interest in how I coped with every aspect of life ... no detail too small. He made me feel special, a one-off, as though he was writing a thesis about me. Though I might not have been a sexual being to Malcolm it is how he made me feel, giving me, however fleeting, moments outside my disability.

A former Jesuit priest, a childhood friend from my days in Mauritius, once told me that if you cannot love yourself how can you expect others to love you. But does this apply if it's not yourself you don't love but your body whilst being content enough with your soul? Can one's body and soul be separated at this level? Back in my early thirties on a reunion in the grounds of Versailles no less I was too busy digesting his statement to vocalise my riposte.

I still don't think I know the answer.

Exit Malcolm was what I did know. And then this foolish virgin did lose his cherry to yet another attached male. Was that my fate? Or was my fate to be worse than that, for regardless of what dribbled out the discharge had been released without protection and Rock Hudson had made the news. THE NEWS! But that ongoing nightmare was not to surface for a month or so. Cleaning myself up and vacating the love nest on a side road off the A1 was the immediate concern as I was advised that his boyfriend would soon be home. Home? It's all complicated, isn't it? And I can remember Malcolm's name but not this fucker's; though I can still visualise his tool. The glorious tricks of the mind. And what does it say about my mind, is memory a choice, or an oblivion chaser? The closest I can aim for is Robert, but I am really not sure and wonder if I am trying to appear less slutty or something by the naming ...

Done if not quite dusted, in fact that's the whole point, for once the dust settled, I was a quivering wreck that expected fate to land a government tombstone on my head. I could not tell Bunny. Well, obviously I could, should have, but chose not to. I did need the reassurances however unscientific theirs would have been, but the price of the disapproval was strangely too high at that juncture. The juncture already being that we had drifted apart as my failure to exit the closet was it seems key to the friendship's continuance. He was not the only gay *friend* who felt this way towards me in the 1980s. Fair enough, we all have our benchmarks, or should it be tidemarks. It did isolate me. Fact. My choice. Fact.

Was there anyone to confide in, there was Carol, from work, a wannabe-fag-hag, but I was too scared of my news being too hot to handle. So, there was no blurting it out. I battled to not let my work suffer as I allowed day-mares to stalk my life.

Anyway, telling Bunny would have been like telling my mother. It wasn't going to happen then. Who do I kid? Myself. I know. I had tried telling my mother, hadn't I? Becoming Judas in my failure. Well, blaming Bunny's influence was easier than accepting that I was mentally ill. Oh! the fundamental minefield. Be Christian Neil, right.

I lived through it. I didn't get the sack, I didn't die

of AIDS, I remained HIV negative. Within months I sold my soul to Maggie's world of Eighties capitalism, changing jobs and diving headlong into fourteen hour working days and stashing the dosh as furtively as a squirrel does his nuts. And it was nuts. But it numbed the feeling of inevitability …

Gradually too, I realised that the return of the monk-cum-nun would survive. And obviously then felt guilty for doing so. Why should my inconsiderate Russian roulette spare me when so many pretty young things were turning ugly before their due time? Plus, AMC was whether I liked it or not, part and parcel of why I survived the last fifteen years of the century. Unscathed. Unloved. Un-fucked. If Bunny had survived because of the strength of Steven's bear hugs then surely, I could place my own down to the grip my disability had on my sexual psyche. Don't raise Malcolm as a contradiction to this take on my life, Malcolm had enjoyed me as a disabled person, as an experiment in itself … and he hadn't been honest with me. As to the cherry-popper, well I always used to assume that it was only single blokes that answered Lonely Hearts advertisements. Naïve an understatement, bloody stupid more like and then so unbelieving.

My visits to the parental home were reducing in number, the tension increasing. To think I had avidly sought an immediate return during my first three years in London. Homosexuality was an English condition; I would be safe if I returned to Scotland. I would not have to endure the same temptations. Oh yes, I would return to the fantasies contained within my bedroom walls, or if daring a walk down Union Street. But time, that great healer, destroyer, egg-timer … the good, the bad and fucked-up … home was no longer in the city's heart but an isolated new-build in the countryside. The three months of right leg op recuperation had shown me what isolation meant, social without even considering the sexual … the sexual of my dreams when it wasn't this body but the body of my same-named fellow pupil that I inhabited to enjoy carnal pleasures. Was that what I wanted a return to. To the domestic friction that I unintentionally added to, for numbering three required sides to be taken, husband or wife, male or female … I did realise that gay son was not an applicable category, let alone acceptable. Even son would, for some years, seem to be tenuous, each departure and return, initially but months apart seemed to accelerate my growing away if only it had also meant my growing up.

The undiagnosed stomach cramps were laid at the door of new potatoes, on the belladonna family principle that some new potatoes were actually not ready for consumption and I was allergically susceptible to being poisoned. Or it could have been rice, we ate an awful lot of rice. Or tension, but was being an Aberdeen football supporter really reason enough?

Fast approaching the age at which both my parents died it is obvious that though they did not embrace the previous generation's dictum that retirement meant death they definitely felt a need for behavioural change. Harsh? I know. I selfishly questioned why they had moved out to beyond the outskirts of Oldmeldrum when they were so intent on retrenching. I should have been grateful that they had moved into a two-bedroomed bungalow. Then, without side-tacking too much, visiting me triggered their final move, to within walking distance of me, upsetting my siblings, but as this is my story …

Was the lack of gratitude all part of the condition called unhappiness. Sexual frustration? Growing pains?

Grow the fuck up, is what someone should have shouted. Slapped me about a bit. Except I would have liked that. STOP IT.

All this happens without me seeing who you see, that is the biggest problem. In isolation I am conditioned to think I am normal. Fine. But actually, not bloody fine for then I am placed with *normal*, the genuinely normal … physically as well as sexually, and my own view of self completely collapses. Thank you and goodnight.

Before I left home in May 1977 my mother had indeed attempted to drill normal into my psyche. She even got Hilda and Betty, from her exclusive circle, the ladies who tended not to gossip within our cul-de-sac, to say the same on those rare occasions when I opened up about having a disability. To state without batting a tray bake away that they did not see me as disabled. Nowadays I would say *bollocks*! Then? Then, I was silently incredulous. How could these three intelligent women all look at me and see normal? Yes, I could grok the fact that they had become accustomed to my physicality but that does not make me normal. It is a disservice to me to state that I am normal on the basis of their habituation. Joe Public does not have this benefit. I would add, furthermore, that my interaction with a blind person would always see their blindness and treat them accordingly. Yes, normally within the context of their blindness. The context is vital.

But how is this helping me get laid? Asked not totally in flippant mode. Though I have always been amazingly relieved that I have never had the sex drive of say rabbits, though that is a gross generalisation … the sex drive of a nympho then … or the pre-coupled Bunny, the human friend not a rabbit … but with some lapin behaviour … and then again, my sex drive appeared greater than flatmate Simon's … and my point is; thank goodness it was not the main behavioural driver of mine.

And to differentiate love from sex. I wish I had had such thoughts as a relatively randy youngster rather than as an ageing, close to seventy-year-old with continence issues as opposed to inappropriate hard-ons. Those were the days. NOT. But again, thankfully not that many and thankfully unremarked at their *inappropriate* occurrence, in heterosexual terms, meant that their visibility was in my eyes not that of the company I was in. Then there's the question of wearing the right sort of underwear, but there's mental digression and then there's mental digression.

Focus!

It's an attempt not to, I know. I know myself.

Too, too well. And the game of self-deceit. It would be all too easy at this point to make-up some fictional romantic love interest to carry the story above and beyond the medical. In the end, however, the fraud would be doing myself as well as you a disservice, regardless of the beautiful poignancy of my fairytale. My life of unrequited barking up the wrong and often straight trees is irrelevant within these pages.

To that I have only one answer, a question in fact. At what point of origin does the apportioning of blame start?

Time to walk away as well as to ponder on all of this, on our lives, past, present and future? Yes, a question, for I can see how it's a mess of knots, as my mother's knitting wool used to end up if she was side tracked by a hiatus on a TV soap opera, when doing the Fair Isle yoke required over one hundred percent of her focus. The pleasure of assisting in the disentangling, the marvelling at how the pattern appeared about the clicking needles, almost at knitting machine speed. How my mother despised Mrs Henderson's knitting machine, *the cheating*. Would I have dared call my mother a Luddite, if I had known the word at that age? Of course not.

Knots! And I want to reference the similarity to my guts and where I eventually ended up after years of misdiagnosis. Years of Colpermin and

Buscopan medication; waste of public funds, prescribed by the laziest GP I have ever come across. So lazy that he could not even converse with original thought but repeated the patients' sentences ... patient *I believe I need a course of antibiotics*, doctor *course of antibiotics*. I ended up seeing a series of locums in preference to seeing him, at least they showed a modicum of interest in a condition most had not come across before. Yes, for my part I had to regurgitate, but it was better than nothing, and one of the things the aborted second foot operation had driven home was the fact that I was no longer a child. Paediatricians were interested in AMC, once you reached adulthood forget it. Yes, you might be an interesting footnote or something you could say you have come across, dealt with, but interest ... talking here about commitment, beginning to end, seeing it through ... forget it.

And the more you age the more it becomes a question of *well what d'you expect me to do about it?* So, you battle, in a guerrilla warfare fashion, small strategic victories like when my toe ulcers were so bad that my private podiatrist sent me to casualty, such his concern about the depth of this particular ulceration. And the surgery had to spring into action as I told the doctors in A&E that my GP practice did not think it was part of their remit. This not only resulted in me being seen every few days for dressing changes by the district nurses at the surgery, and subsequently weekly podiatry visits but also a switch from paying for my footwear to having it supplied by the NHS. The last private pair cost over £1,700.

My NHS podiatry had stopped back at the end of the last century. I used to be seen up in Westminster, occasioned by my initial place of employment. The title of the novel *Twelve o'Clock Feet* originates from my preferred appointment time once I moved to City employment, attempting to squeeze it within the lunchbreak. Fine and dandy until podiatry became a local authority healthcare issue and I was not a resident, a local worker did not count and I fell out of the system ... but I could afford to pay, so I did locally, attending a clinic on Saturday mornings either before or after the weekly Sainsbury's shop, depending on when I got out of bed.

Slipstream

So, I tootle off to work in the City of London, using the hours to bury my sexuality to all but a few … and by the end of the century I had finally stopped kidding myself that bi was remotely feasible. Apologies all round.

By which time both my parents had died and I was left with two aunts and a Godmother who, according to my mother, would be scandalised if I was homosexual. Thus, my sexual deceit remained until their generation did not. Totally my choice, not my deceased mother's to make.

I also do know, and appreciate, that despite this weakness in self-identity declaration that the strengths I do have also stem from her desire for normalcy for this son … if we could have a conversation now Mum?

At the end of the Eighties fifteen months of loose stool could neither be diagnosed nor ended. At the time, the only additional information the medical profession could provide was that I had an extra loop of tubing within my intestine. Thirty centimetres perchance? Thank you!

My own urban myth was that it had been started by the over indulgence in my plum tree glut and arrested by an over indulgence of Christmas cake. One appears somewhat less likely than the other – my myths, your choice.

Through all these years I continued to experience the immobilising stomach cramps. When they hit, they knocked me out. On a couple of occasions, I was so badly knocked out that I awoke to my bowels having opened in my stupor … a little known portend of things to come.

The diagnosis shifted to pressure of work,

though this did not fit with when the cramps occurred during holidays or entertaining dinner guests.

Retiring at fifty should have also alleviated the issue but it didn't. And it wasn't down to repressing my sexuality as I had finally come out to Karen and Kevin and Louise and Paul upon retirement, to my new tennis club members from 2007 and Tony and Sue G and anyone else who knew me via Current TV's documentary *I'm coming out* in 2010.

The cramps may have been less prevalent but when they occurred, they were reaching new levels of ferocity. After one bout too many and a particularly severe one at that (which I retrospectively realised had included faecal vomiting) I gave in to Sue G's insistence and attended her homeopathic clinic, which I insisted on calling homo-pathetic, and succumbed to the prognosis that I was lactose intolerant, for it was from the time of the return to Scotland that I starting drinking at least half-a-pint of milk a day. I say succumbed for there was to my mind a tad of a seance like approach to the homeopathy diagnosis, suggestions made to trigger reactions. But I fell for it and followed a lactose free diet for the three years prior to my January 2020 hospitalisation. Anything to relieve the doubling-up agony of the cramps.

Anxiety did often appear as the common denominator, whether work or social or physical activity related. I am sure it did have a part to play but the main cause remained arthrogryposis multiplex congenita.

Ready, steady, go …

August 2021

Am I always trying to rewrite my past? Isn't that what we all do? Revisionists! Where experience throws a new light on the past, how others (and perhaps you) behaved and you can forgive others and excuse yourself.

Guilty. I am always revising my view of my parents. Perhaps, just perhaps, this will stop though, as I approach the age that they died. Somehow, I doubt it, for as I still read and thus learn about myself I continue to reassess my child-parent relationship.

And the crossroad moments of life. Oh yes, retrospective crossroads. And this particular retrospective places me as an emotional as well as physical coward. The wishful thinking of looking back, it was as if I had wanted to suck him into the safety of my oxygen filled tent when the outside was filled with the walking dead, blemished bodies soon to die of euphemistic pneumonia. A teenage vagrant, at risk? At risk of being picked up by a predator?

But I picked up neither this particular Tuesday night waif and stray, nor any subsequent one, in the underpass beneath Waterloo Bridge. They would have been a possession too far, too close, and the motive was intrinsically wrong, even if I thought I'd be saving them from HIV infection. Stick to cats!

Funny, as in strange, but it was the fear of being viewed as a predator that actually governed my behaviour. Crazy I'd admit to, but not mad. I already appreciated the soulless quality of possessions in relation to my well-being.

Yes, I did sort of care what others thought … actually, far, far too much if truth be told. Take someone from work, like Tony, we would both have been classed as equally boring salarymen if we had been Japanese. He supported the Arsenal, I didn't. He was married, I wasn't. He had number three child on the way, I had an internal fiction of might have been.

You'd make a good dad had been stated, loosely by? By far too many, but it was not a statement I sought out. It was not what I was about.

I can no longer remember the play I had seen at the National Theatre when I stopped for the briefest flicker of a moment, almost imperceptible with my gait, but enough for his face to linger forever! But I walked on under Waterloo Bridge to the station, my balls in no way big enough for whatever might have ensued. I kept on walking even as I thought of turning back and offering him the requested bed for the night. A discard from up north. That's my fairytale, and I'll stick to it. That simple.

Actually, not that simple, as this was before mobiles and emails, and I was but a self-confessed neuter spectator on life. Did my disability make me seem less dangerous, a soft touch, a mug? Apart from sheer cowardice I have also wondered, over time, whether I felt unclean at how now a London habitué I was a predator in sheep's clothing. Yes, milliseconds of over thinking.

I went back the following night and he wasn't there, but the face and hoodie remain to this day. But one of this life's loose ends. Meaning diddly-squat to all but me. Yet to me it remains a seminal moment of path choosing. To me. If he survives is there a chance, he might read this. Sadly, however, this isn't fiction.

Time! Now, I do remember, the play at the National was *Pravda*, that's the truth, at least, that's my recall.

Funny, I am trying to put my tale into context for you before literally spilling my guts, or having my guts spilled, exposed, whatever.

Glib! Flippancy! Whatever to that too …

And in so doing, or attempting to, I realise how unblack and white it is. It is so much easier to clean up the stoma's effluent than recall all my past.

I want a family. The end. Retrospective

flippancy. But it still hurts, but I shall be honest, a sting … not as the hurt was as the time, over ten years ago, when it was devastation. That's when my guts were ripped out emotionally. When I thought all sorts of things, so many unpleasant things. I was already old. Look how I would grimace at having to attend friends' family gatherings, my hearing wasn't what it used to be and I found the surround sound difficult to deal with, trying to isolate conversation threads directed at me. I had, sadly, lost my tolerance for allowing the under-fives the attempt to straighten my fingers. *Open your hands Uncle Neil.* Was that it? The catalyst. But a deep trough, and there, I'm up the other side

Oh, how it does revolve, if you're thinking that I have done the grand tour reflecting on … round and around, anticlockwise as well as clockwise, you are spot on. Had I had children?

*

You don't necessarily know what is percolating within, neither emotionally nor physically. Disconcerting when it all appears or sounds like the norm, perhaps being played in a slightly different key that you yourself can't discern enough to be concerned about. Or is there any change? Is it just retrospectively you feel there must have been, something that you didn't notice.

Simon died less than twelve months since our last meeting. What's that all about? COVID! Oops, I've mentioned the pandemic word so soon. Its legacy does have a lot to answer for, even if not the ALL that the likes of hospitals and your local doctor's surgery would lay at COVID's door.

As I was thinking that I should have cancelled. But cancelling was something that I didn't do. I now wonder whether he had been thinking the same. How was it we were suddenly old. We had met a couple of years earlier. Upright men. At least in demeanour. Simon was as private as I was regarding *private life* with no nudge-nudge, wink-wink intended from either of us. We had never opened up with regards to emotions that were other than basically filial in content. Whilst I had *come out*, he hadn't and all I assumed from what he didn't say, as much as from what he did, was that he was just further down the asexual route that I had started to more and more, shrink-wrap myself in.

Binary? Now that single word takes me right back, all the way back to the days in my maths class. I had moved up from the dunces, a tad and Mrs Howard was one of the great teachers, given a group of us lesser achievers to work on. Some of us did. The sort of problem solving I enjoyed. Funny, as thoughts go off on a tangent, how I hated physics but passed the exams; loved chemistry but couldn't pass an exam for toffee. And as for maths, I was a slow burner and Mrs Howard found the ignition spark. Or so this side view, from the distance of a fire door leads me to believe.

And I am losing focus. Again!

So, Simon was also not one hundred percent. What is one hundred percent when you reach your mid to late sixties? Even for Mr Blue Sky …

Is one hundred percent where you accept certain physical and mental restraints as givens and you no longer think of them as issues to be considered worthy of a mention in answer to *how are you?* however rhetorical the asking is?

But there was an underlying relief when I realised

Stoma in a teacup

that he wouldn't feel I was deserting him when I initiated the end of our day out at Nymans, exaggerated relief (or not) when I sat in my car and headed for home. Wishful thinking, retrospectively, otherwise just more ignorance is more bliss than considering this is the beginning of something.

But for Simon it was the beginning of a premature end. It's all very well his GP being distraught. It's all very well Simon liking his GP. Fuck it! It isn't very well at all. COVID has, like it or not, and I don't, allowed the vast majority of the medical profession to hide from us, the patients. Yes, some will quote guidelines, but they are guidelines … why don't they know their patients. Simon and his GP obviously knew each other yet the extent of the misdiagnosis seems grotesque. Arthritis in his right hip when it was actually lung cancer, the latter finally diagnosed three weeks before his death as the cancer had enjoyed an uninterrupted traipse throughout his body. For fuck's sake! So, the likeable GP feels remorse …

Oh yes, Simon is guilty. Like I am. But sometimes you do need to cry wolf. There's a place for stoicism, but not when you live on your own and changes are so marginally incremental as to appear no change at all. It's where you need to have family and friends who feel they can be open with you and say you look shit. It's all so easier said than done. Eventually Simon's sister took charge, but far too late, not her fault. The circumstantial blame rests with Simon, and what historically he had allowed as family intrusion. Intrusion? Oh! how one's private self can give such life-threatening airs and graces to themselves.

And I can't say, not hand on heart anyway, whether it would have been any different, in my case, if I had had someone ... as I avoided telling my mother *stuff* likewise, I avoided telling my nearest and dearest ... HERE! Or, if I had been there?

I know what I want to say. That it would have made diddly-squat of a difference by then. But the *by then* is purely bitter bile and not at my friends, but at me. And wrong, on all counts, acceptable or not. So there! Am I as bad, as Simon? Is it a single person thing? A single male thing? I don't think sexual orientation or delineation comes into it. Thank goodness, how complicated that would be nowadays if I thought it did and have to tiptoe through that particular modern minefield.

I think, and I do occasionally. I think that we as in Western culture have swung too far in the application of gender choice, and quite unintentionally have given the youth of today quite a different conundrum from that my generation was contending with. Looking, that is, at each post Second World War decade, and the liberation of women alongside sexual freedom for both sexes.

And, obviously, STOP right there. Both sexes! Are there just two? I did do German at school, good old *das* for the neuter. *Das Mädchen* always used to give me some sort of perverse comfort, along the lines of if Germans think of girls as *it* then perhaps, just perhaps, I don't need to over worry about not being quite the *him* I should be.

Fill up a survey and the options of F or M have multiplied. And, to be perfectly honest, I fail to understand. And, yes, another *and*, and I don't particularly want to. Not in a denial sense. Be who we are. But more in a labelling sense. Make sense?

September 2021

On occasion I wonder if I triggered it. Me, myself, I! Reflux unannounced … there it is in your mouth, on your lips, out come the thoughts if not the words. Wrong audience? You are walking by an eye-catching DILF, pushchair ahead of him. And the nasty thought occurs, immediate guilt, too late, the imagined speech bubble is there, as you address the child. *Hello Sonny, did you know that your Dad and I used to fuck.* Jesus! What is the matter with you? You know you would never say that. Perish the thought; even though you've had it.

Stoma in a teacup

You shudder. Wish you weren't who you are. Want to lose having had the thought. Oh, that most impossible of all wishes.

So where did the thought spring from, was it actually even related to someone in the first, second or third instance? No. It was a lust directed at a young father taking his son out, a more common sight now, since the first year of COVID. Habits were changing, even if my behaviour wasn't.

That isn't and isn't meant to be funny.

I have always been one of those who believes that positive thoughts are a vital part of keeping physically well.

Don't tell me frolicking with young married men is a healthy thought. Well, actually it could be if left at that. Extrapolating to the extent of being a releasing physical as well as mental exercise could be construed as very healthy. Self-deception, he wrote.

Retrospection. The repeating of mistakes, mainly because they never appeared as mistakes. They weren't mistakes. It was you living your life. Even if one of imaginings, of unfulfilled wishes, daydreaming. Shit happens and not all roads lead to happy endings, just you wait till you turn the page to October 2021! Take nothing for granted and be grateful for those constants in your life. For those who don't necessarily live in your pocket but are there, available, on call even. I even have this inner one-way thought transference with certain friends. Knowing they would be there for me is enough, so I explain my issues, thoughts, worries telepathically. Is that a pathetic con? Yes, sometimes I do wonder if it is, whether I am kidding myself, whether if the push came to shove, they would actually be there ... hand holding or lending me an ear. But because I am there for them and others (some would say all comers) I feel a certain confidence that they would be for me, thus the lack of the need to test it. The mere knowledge enough comfort, that warm oozy feeling of being cared for. Go figure, I guess, if it's never occurred to you. In which case, I feel sorry for you, it's one of life's treasures, knowing these disparate angels have you in their thoughts.

Meanwhile, within, the internal mechanics of my body that is, not the madcap cerebral pulses, things are going array without me appreciating to what extent ... where you carry on affecting normality, putting on a brave face, mainly because you don't actually realise how brave you are being. If you did it would actually be classed as foolhardy.

Like the last time I saw Simon alive, at Nymans. I should have cancelled but I am retrospectively glad I didn't even though I had no idea that despite my year ahead in age it would be him that death would actually visit first. I was feeling bloated with intermittent stomach cramps, neither the sitting posture of the drive, nor the walk around the grounds helping. Whilst Simon's health, never really robust since retirement, appeared better than on our previous random meeting, he was having issues with his walking, though was positive about the improvement to his well-being and pocket that the cessation of smoking had generated. Was Simon even worse than me at kidology?

Interesting what you do have in common with someone from your past, as to whether it's just the past or is there present and any future in it. My own test, as the listener, is to whether they in turn are listening to you. Are they interested enough to ask any questions, and by this I don't just mean of the superficial *how are you* sort? Yes, you revisit what you shared and the conversation extends from there, at times questioning each other's recall, the tricks of memory, confusing each other with different characters from the historic jigsaw. Missing pieces. Separate but together?

But there is no together, I have no together. No two.

And whose fault is that? My least favourite of all my rhetorical questions.

*

Since leaving home doing as I'm told has never featured that highly in my life. Though as my sixties draw to an end, I do notice that I am somewhat more apt at listening than I was before, and sometimes, yes occasionally, I actually follow said advice. Then there's regretting doing so. Take a man bag for example, and please, please take mine. Okay, in principle I agree, how sensible for someone like me, to have a handbag. But ladies, the gravity principle that applies to your handbags equally applies to my man bag and with my AMC fingers I end up silently screaming in frustration as I struggle to extract keys or train pass or theatre tickets or mobile phone from their respective slender compartments. Oh! to return to the joy of the plastic carrier bag, and yes, where gravity was as extant but the right-hand claw could rummage more freely. But until the somewhat homosexual looking man bag disintegrates, I shall continue to sling it over my neck in arched frustration. So camp, in unseen moments – eh mirror?

The avoidance of camp acts highlighted within the domain of the Bunny friendship, where that stage was solely his, and as such was a metre by which my own behaviour was mine to fathom and act upon, knowing how uncomfortable I felt at any high-pitched drama, however much of a show it was. Why act, I would question with a shudder as the one loathing any focus of attention drawn to self. Look the other way, I'm a cripple not a dancing queen. Please! And I know Bunny would often do it in public, so as to make his personal audience squirm, and we did, whilst enchanting the general public by playing-up to type.

Not for me. No, not in shame, just in inclination. And, it must be said, in some alarm too, for the thoughts did occur that wrong place, wrong time and Bunny could end up in danger … though I calmed myself with the thought that all this high camp was an act for his current entourage not Joe Public, so that when on his tod he portrayed a somewhat calmer personage. Well, that was my hope. And for sure it was my own design, so much so that I would catch myself completely off guard if I squealed at anything.

Trying to think back, back to my days since actually coming out … have I been less guarded, has my out life allowed an automation to my behaviour, where it is no longer sanctioned by qualms of third-party interpretation. A who-gives-a-fuck mentality? There definitely is some of that within the freedom that being out brought to my life. My freedom of expression roaming freer that ever before. Still not Bunny-camp though. Bless him, I may laugh, grin or smile – thank you to him for having his nature, his uninhibited disposition, allowing us less unconstrained souls a vicarious promenade through certain passages of life.

No, I shall not stroll along that gravel path today,

the noise grates and my toes are sore.

Empathy! Actually, a fucking total lack of it, and this before I am acutely ill. Almost two years before the stoma joy I was admitted to hospital with an intestine blockage. Which a laxative shifted, and was the catalyst to me shifting from one doctor's surgery to another. Apart from poo-pooing my claims of having a blockage my former doctor phoned me the day after my hospital admittance to tell me to go to A&E as they had found a blockage. Thanks Doc! Years of misdiagnosis, stating that what I had was IBS and the placebo treatment dispensed, Colpermin or Buscopan, when all along it was an AMC idiosyncrasy. Obvious if you can be bothered looking. And don't start me off with dear Dr Raj. I said, don't start me off with dear Dr Raj.

So, back to the lack of empathy and the chap to my left in my four-bed side ward. He has a visit from a couple of the medical staff. The subsequent privacy awarded to the conversation they were about to have with him, and him on his own, was to draw the curtains around his bed. That the privacy. Really? Yes. I was in no way privy to anything that had passed before between the three participants to what I was about to overhear ... BUT! To my big ears, it sounds like without any preamble they ask him whether his affairs are all in order and if not, he should get a move on and make arrangements with his local hospice. I kid you not. If I was in shock, how was he feeling? What was he feeling? He had a wife or partner, could the medics not have made sure that she was there. Had patient and hospital staff had a relationship I was not party to? But even so. Was this really how you broke the news? Notice of death. I had not been an in-patient long enough to be in a striking up a casual conversation with, he was more often than not away from his bed, returning with a coffee, I imagined he enjoyed a cheeky cigarette once his coffee was purchased. And I was too busy minding Rod's business across from me; either from the perspective of his camp gay great-nephew's visits or from how the staff mistreated him as a result of his deafness and their unwillingness to compromise. The fourth side ward occupant was the most normal, advising how he had been hours from death when his internal bleeding was stemmed in the nick of time. He was pleased to see I was on the mend. He was referring to the racket I had made upon my arrival on the ward as I was assaulted with having a catheter fitted as well as a tube inserted via my nose into my upper stomach to remove any remaining gunge from my faecal vomiting from the week before.

I am sure you'd like to hear about faecal vomiting! Off to the Royal Opera House as a New Year treat with my friend Ed I disembarked at London Bridge and returned home, double-up in pain, whilst frothing bile. As that night progressed to tomorrow, I eventually vomited faeces that could not exit through the normal channel. Not to be put on anyone's bucket list, though a bucket at hand is somewhat useful.

The nurse, given the implementation, basically told me to man-up and not be such a wuss as I squirmed and vocally resisted what she, to my mind, did with unnecessary vigour. I would say enjoyment but that might, even for me, be an exaggeration. Might. She had to use a thinner plastic tube for the nose job, ironically. So, on that basis alone, go figure whether I was exaggerating or not.

Perhaps if I had been really ill ill, as opposed to merely being in need of remedial action to the latest bout of faecal vomiting, my resistance to both would have been less and therefore her job would have been easier and the application of both would have occurred with me slipping in and out of physical awareness as caressing drugs coursed my body.

On a business trip to Japan, I had a severe enough attack of pharyngitis to warrant hospital admission. Apart from the comic strip aspect of not being able to speak because of the pharyngitis, no-one spoke English, and here they were having to deal with a disabled and dribbling *gaijin*. Thankfully the health centre had given me a covering note, which had also been useful in the taxi as I on occasion caught the driver's look of *what the* in his mirror at the slobbering wreck trying to hold it together whilst being unable to swallow. Apart from mildly amusing myself at the recall my point is that that was one of the first times in my life where I have been so ill as to consciously have felt the benefit of medication courses through my body. I felt that weak upon admission that a rag doll would have had more of a spinal column. There would have been no point in vocally abusing me with the Japanese equivalent of *man-up* as I was the ideal putty state nurses like, malleable. Oh! if only I had been in that state of readiness for the nurse at the PRUH. I assume, though obviously there was no explanation given, that I was being prepped for an operation should the dosage of laxative not clear the intestinal blockage. Wearing a catheter meant that when the sluice gates opened, I needed assistance with bottom wiping, having a tube up *me* nose and one out of my penis somewhat disabled me. I know, I am a laugh.

It was a shame, not, that the staff nurse had to do the bottom-wiping and not Nurse Ratched, though the latter would undoubtedly have used sandpaper to clean me up.

The laxative having worked we can now fast forward from January 2020 to October 2021 … missing out eighteen months of life with COVID.

October 2021

The day before the day my world ended was reasonably eventful, dramatic even! Well, a queen is allowed a smidge of a drama, surely? We were at the height of the fuel shortage, real or consumer driven. Real to us who were running low. I was running low and had a drive to Selhurst and back scheduled for that lovely balmy October afternoon. My mileometer said I had thirty-five miles left in the tank. That's plenty for a twenty-mile round trip. Right? A fifteen-mile safety net for traffic hold ups, especially when being decanted off of Warminster Road onto South Norwood's High Street. There definitely was plenty left in the adrenalin tank after the mighty Eagles came back from two-nil down to claim a deserved draw against Leicester City.

No garages I passed on the return journey had any juice left in their tanks and I made it back to my glove-fitting of a garage with seventeen miles left on the clock. Trying to drive fuel efficiently had become a bit of an art form on both legs of the journey.

The local Shell garage had had petrol when I drove by on my outbound journey, but it also had a queue. By the use of my hands free, safety first, mobile I did advise Ed, Sue H and Val of the availability and queue …

The day before!

How true that we don't know what will happen next, let alone the next day. The coming week was supposed to see me fly to Aberdeen for a couple of nights with friends and a catch-up with my brothers. This trip one of the COVID-19 postponements from 2020.

The next day?

Just NEXT!

*

I suppose part of me had always wondered what it would be like to dial 999. And then to actually do it on your own behalf and ask for ambulance as the service too.

To know that it was an emergency without the need for referral, very unlike me. Previously I'd always needed my friends Karen or Sue G, principally them, occasionally others, telling me to go to the doctors, take ABC vitamins or do XYZ exercises. That sort of thing. Give me free, one hundred per cent, unsought advice.

It was a normal day.

It was a normal Monday; where I am single in fact as well as in my own fiction. So, I ask again, any woke ticks for this status?

Upon waking I feed Gizzy the cat and fill up the kettle, which I then switch on before face washing and teeth brushing. Thus, a normal every second Monday begins. Every second Monday morning I hit tennis balls for an hour from eight o'clock with Mikhail. I could wax unlyrically about how tennis is so not the sport I should have taken up, but I did, and love it. For the record, and I have always wanted to state it, I have always played against able bodied humans. Just for the record, you understand ... nothing to do with the story. I magic inclusivity even before it's a desirable element on tick lists.

Arthrogryposis multiplex congenita is my own abracadabra! Well deserving of its bold tick in current perceptions and understandings.

As that fateful Monday progressed still no real sign of what was percolating within. As midday approached Bill and Ben would have arrived late for two hours of gardening. Even whilst gardening with them I recall no twinges on that mild early autumn day. Did any cramps start after I more than likely gulped down my sandwich lunch in readiness for the arrival of the Geberit saleswoman? She was going to be demonstrating the fancy new toilet I anticipated having installed as my current bathroom was converted into a wet-room. I think perhaps they had started, for sure she did not receive my full attention.

It was definitely after her departure that I took to bed, and from what I remember, not long after that I telephoned Ed and advised that I did not think our Monday night curry would be occurring that evening. Recall?

It was when I stood up to feed Gizzy that I realised I was in trouble, real trouble. I was having trouble breathing if upright. The cat fed I collapsed back onto my bed and nursed the cramping. The usual, telling myself each shooting stab of pain meant one less to endure. And I believed it until the next knitting needle jab pierced my resistance and I screamed.

An excursion to the toilet confirmed the breathing issue. This was a new symptom that had not previously occurred alongside the stomach cramps, and though short-lived cramping had occurred in August and September this was something else, and reminded me of my January 2020 hospital admission.

But the breathing, the lack of being able to unless lying down? I had had breathing issues for ten or so years, which tended to be manageable (especially if I remained calm and didn't talk) usually dissipated once I had been to toilet if not before. Although the diagnostics with regards to the constriction to my diaphragm were not to become apparent until the summer of 2022.

But this? This was my first such episode of stomach cramps affecting my breathing.

Stopping my ability to breathe.

I was scared.

My mobile was on my bed as I thought I might have to cancel the curry date. And now … at 18:59 and flat out on my bed I dialled 999 …

*

I apologised to Paul. It's what I did. What we do. Isn't it?

So, I apologised, until the next time and the next apology …

I had called him this side of midnight and he had returned my call from the other side.

Life saver? I had advised the doctor that I wanted to live, resuscitate … Paul as witness.

Technology! But don't ask me to recall. 11:59, the closest you could get before PM changed back to AM all over again.

The phone's record states that the call was made at 11:59, I could not recall, and vaguely his return call seven minutes later.

There was a very good reason for me not remembering that 11:59 call, it wasn't made by me, but by the doctor. Have they not heard of ICE, sorry Paul, doubly sorry Karen. Sorry Tony. Sorry EVERYONE.

(I made a promise not to swear. A promise is a promise.)

Now for the doctor to have made the call I must have been able to access the phone's innards by tapping in the four-digit password, for future reference it's the house number repeated.

So why Paul?

So why Paul? I know, I just asked that. But it would be impossible for me to ask the doctor who made the call as I would not be able to identify him, a fly-by-night. Said doctor's first question was the resuscitation one. I said *no* then changed my mind. Is sixty-seven old? Talking about nowadays not my parents' days. It was the changing of my mind that made him grab my phone. *I've a right one here*, he probably thought, or the equivalent idiom in his language and culture. That's not just me and inbuilt prejudice, prejudices. Paul said he had trouble understanding him which is why he called back seven minutes later ... according to my mobile phone records, the truth, the whole truth and nothing but the truth.

To be honest, and why shouldn't I be, that day was regulation normal for a Monday ... hello-ish Tuesday!

*

What had I not been told? The operation was on Wednesday the 6th after the failure of the medicated laxative to unblock my pipes on Tuesday the 5th.

What had I not been told on the 5th or the 6th was that I could awake from the blockage clearance operation with my stoma as a new outer-body experience. Or had I? Was I so ill that it had not registered? I do remember asking if they couldn't try another dose of the laxative, after all it had worked in January 2020.

Had I not been told, according to my recall, because they did not know? I know that during subsequent *private* consultations with my surgeon Mary-Jane, she told me that my AMC innards were laid out to their own specification not that of a regular (see how I avoid *normal*) human being ... for instance my liver sat above my groin.

I am not stating all this as though I would have refused to sign off on the consent forms if I had known what I was to wake up with. It would have, perhaps, for it's all hypothetical, given me pause for thought.

But I honestly cannot remember, even though I deep down believe it is something I would have remembered, however ill I was the day before the operation.

*

As clear thinking as that may retrospectively be

post-op the morphine had kicked in …

There were two views on offer, apart from the chap in the bed diagonally opposite, escaped as he had from the fall of Kabul. It sounded a lot to me like my former colleague Chuck's description of the fall of Saigon … but it hadn't been morphine that Chuck's brother had been on.

The scene was becoming somewhat crowded … and the morphine offered but two views. Remember? Yet, I only wished to forget.

The colourful option was quartered, blue, yellow, brown and green. The monochrome one was just that, I suppose; and I was in one of three cots. Can I draw it for you? It was at Paul and Louise's. Well, I thought it was. It wasn't, obviously. But that's what I imagined.

The cot further away than the other one was against a partition wall. Half plasterboard half glass, the other side a corridor that appeared to have a regular figure pace it from close to far at set intervals. If only I could focus on the time lapse but my bandages were in the way. At any rate that's what happened when I started to unravel them and subsequently took to tugging at the tubing.

The colourful option occurred if I closed my eyes. Oil and water caught together between two layers of glass, except not. It was like a giant traybake, roughly quartered in that the colours ran at the edges, but did not mingle. A not quite set harlequin brownie; obviously brown in one quarter with the other three being blue, yellow and green. Loose shapes and designs would rise up from the surface but not breakthrough.

What a trip, but I wanted it to stop. It was real you see, not my imagination. This bloody mess was all too real …

On two consecutive nights I had to be rescued from my misguided attempts to escape from my confines, be it removing the stoma bag and removal of the range of drips attached to my body. Tying myself and the tubes in knots in the process. Both occasions coming too, in some sort of sense, stating to nurse Brian, a most gentle sloth, that I didn't want to die. On both nights the same staff nurse had been totally disinterested in my suicide attempts. I didn't actually want to die; I merely wanted the nightmares to stop.

Stoma in a teacup

I didn't want to be stalking the nursery in Paul and Louise's house like some Egyptian mummy, this one clarted in blood. The blood grey as opposed to red in this monochrome environment, where I was the only one on the move … other than the corridor ghost. The children must have been asleep in the cots. What if they woke and I scared them? Would Paul think I was doing it on purpose, then the shift, back to the brownie …

My world of four colours was a living breathing one, sentient to at least itself. I could not work out where the four mouths were. I assumed they had one each, though it was the brown that I saw, understood to be a mouth. The others were mobile swamp-like creations, I wouldn't say creatures as their extent was limited by the space that my mind's eye saw them occupy, rectangular, almost square.

Visions of morphine.

Tony saved me. I could not handle a third night of Neil unplugged, with the attendant scenarios. Though it was days later before I fully appreciated that the whole Kabul, spy, gunfire and police in the corridor story had also been fuelled by morphine. I knew I could count on Tony to use one of his more forceful modes to ensure that morphine was removed from my drug cocktail.

No more hallucination nightmares.

Now just the real ones of the future, the reality of a stoma bag, the reality of the extent of the operation. How to get back on to your two feet.

Gay written all over it? Of course not, but I do like it as my default button. Regardless of exhaustion I enjoy the fact that the hyacinths have a smell which my nose detects, as opposed to enjoying the intrinsic scent of hyacinths, which I don't enjoy. And my vase of daffodils sends out its own scent, less strong but distinctive and very there.

This is the conundrum, perhaps paradox of the lesser me, the diminished me.

*

Two weeks in hospital, and though aware of my morphine nightmares I was not, thankfully, aware of how, if at all, disruptive I was at night. But by the second week night time sleep was virtually impossible. And if you tried daytime catch-up the staff assumed you were unwell. Well perhaps one member of staff did.

In my four-bed side ward there was always a nightbird geriatric, sometimes one that needed twenty-four/seven surveillance. The night staff seemed to find this harder to do than the day staff. At times, okay OFTEN I did wonder how many of the night staff had day jobs and really wanted to have a kip … hey, I'm sick in bed and can't get to sleep why should you … especially when paid to stay awake. As for the Filipino night staff … not all … TOTALLY not all. But the abusers sure abused. One of the youngsters on the alleged twenty-four/seven surveillance was too busy monitoring his mobile phone twenty-four/seven, others were enjoying what sounded like Filipino YouTube videos – *tumahimik ka! I-off ito!* Pretty please. I witnessed others taking their breaks irrespective of the staff nurse's wishes, this particularly obvious when the staff nurse was of Afro-Caribbean ethnicity.

Thank goodness I was being kept awake for otherwise how would I be able to report all this to you. Is the reporting of inter-racial prejudice by a white Brit woke?

One of the other things that I found somewhat odd on my ward was that there were often more night staff (doing diddly squat) than day staff (rushed off their feet). Hello management!

*

As today's visitor left I would stupidly try to snuggle down into my hospital bed as if it was mine at home. That was a short, sharp reminder of where I was … in all senses. I was not back home, cosied-up with Gizzy, enjoying warm reminisces. No siree, I was not only still in hospital, still coming to terms with what any future would hold but also as restless as ever on a bed that could be shaped any which way but comfortable.

Exasperation took hold, the benefit of the visit fading all too fast. A stoma. A giant out of body blob, incarcerated in a bag, for the *healthy* deep pink wobbly thing had an opening at its base, for the release of one's excrement. Would I ever come to terms with this? I couldn't but help myself think of it. It was there. I was there. Supporting another life form. Was determination to succeed in bag changing enough it itself? Timing was such a big part of the process. Or so you thought till the next out of sync volcano. *Don't let the bag get so full.* Oh, thank you so much for the advice. Dear Stoma Bag, did you hear that, Nurse Cindy would like you not to fill up so that cleaning me and changing you can be a much easier job. I dare not tell Cindy the response I received.

Another fitful night of dozing with the bed opposite still fighting off life as opposed to death. Though I did feel I knew where he was at. I was relieved that wherever his head was at he would not realise that the nurse on watch actually wasn't. Well, he was on watch, watching something on his mobile as the glow was all too visible through the curtain screening that they had pulled around the bed to reduce the distraction for us three fighting to sleep as opposed to die.

When I volunteered for the 2017 World Athletic Championships, I was inclined to advise my fellow volunteer, Nicole, that I was writing a report. Subsequently anything that happened would be appended by me as *going into my report*. It helped pass a lot of the downtime that occurred during the volunteering sessions.

*

As for the day the hospital ran out of baked potatoes. I say day, it was days ... I was discharged on the third day of the potato famine ... by which time there was also a shortage of other favourite meals and puddings.

The whole food choice game in hospitals needs reviewing. The menus walk. And one of my guesses at why baked potatoes ran out, apart from bad quarter mastering, is that when asked what you want and don't have a menu in front of you baked potato is the first choice offered, so it's the remembered choice or if nothing sinks in the patient goes *the first one*.

What is and isn't allowed? Nil by mouth is very clear, and only liquids is also reasonably clear ... but otherwise?

How come the doctors themselves aren't aware that the hospital doesn't do toast? Every morning I'd be ready to cringe when the doctors were doing their rounds. Without fail the doctors who tended Donald across from me said he

Stoma in a teacup

could now have something plain like toast. I loved the plain sandwiches, the packs said *handmade especially for you* two slices of dry bread with a slice of ham or cheese inserted. I can't believe it's not butter doesn't even get a look in – nothing but a slice of ham or cheese. Be thankful, I say. It's marvellous, and less fat too.

I had to leave the ubiquitous carrots and broccoli on the side of my plate every meal, but there was no-one who would have grabbed a hold of my fork to arrest a carrot being illegally eaten. Well Cindy might have … but Cindy would have done it in aid of general table manners. Once allowed solids and a meal that required a knife and fork Cindy thought I needed re-educating on the use of cutlery. What part of her nursing role had made her fail to realise that I had AMC. It was Cindy who was convinced that I had two left foot boots – she could never figure out which boot was which, to such an extent that I started to doubt myself!

Still on food, it was basically a question of eat or starve, no-one had the time or inclination to ensure that you ate your ordered meal. The catering staff removed trays at set visits. I

97

personally experienced hanging on to my pudding plate *I haven't finished.*

Suggestion, each side ward has a laminated menu that capable patients are apprised of prior to decision time, as the menu only changes twice – summer menu, winter menu. Have the menus be specific to needs, diets, allergies … ethnicity is fine but also condescending as well as exclusive as opposed to inclusive. No-one, absolutely not one member of staff ever assisted me with my menu choice once I was allowed solids, unless I specifically asked, which I did in the early days when I was allowed the *handmade especially for you* sandwiches.

A topic worthy of further air time …

*

BUT!

*

And I am back home … finally discharged once the hospital received the call confirming that the care package was in place.

I was in the bathroom; little did I know that I would soon be taking up residence within it. Flippancy will get you nowhere. Not long home from hospital. Less than an hour. Even from the bathroom, with the door closed, I could discern confrontation and wondered who dare argue with my friend Sue G.

The combatant's name was Kim, head observer. Proclaimed head observer. Her and her team weren't carers. Let's be clear on that. Yes, let's! Oh yes! I know, this was the Bromley Home Care Package in action but without the care. 'We don't care,' said Kim, oblivious to the content of that particular soundbite within the context of her presence. 'We observe.'

Was this Kim showing-off as she was in training mode? Sadly, Kim was unable to observe that the princess was seemed as unimpressed with her training as much as the job itself as she examined her beautiful manicured fingernails. Her aquamarine eyeshadow fascinated me, blinking like a chameleon from a Disney cartoon.

Kim was defining, mostly to Sue G, I was after all only the patient, and disabled, bless … Kim was defining all they did as observers and how quickly they would desist once they observed that I could. Care? No Neil, listen – OBSERVE!

Three observation house-calls a day, basically meal times … with a huge margin for error … as I was to discover. I thought I heard 7-9, 12-2 and 6-8. Thinking is no good.

Nor is flippancy, but sometimes both occur.

Before leaving Kim announced that she needed to check my blood pressure, temperature and oxygen levels to ensure that I didn't require an immediate return to hospital. What? Over my dead body! That can be arranged. Oh yes, the hospital holy trinity of obs. Thankfully I was allowed to remain in my home.

The observers' *can't-do* list was obviously extensive … other than no help whatsoever particular reference was made to the fact that though Kim herself had stoma experience most of her girls didn't. Obviously not Jean Brodie girls.

Okay! Enough.

Can I describe Kim as a hardnosed bitch? A face

more freckled and more lined than mine with no volume control over her vocal cords. Or the volume was used as a control.

Goodnight!

Sue G and I looked at each other speechless; was that really the care package that I couldn't leave hospital until it had been put in place?

It was only then, as we both drew breath that Sue G told me that she had to remove a dead rat of a gift courtesy of Gizzy upon arrival at my home ... and I know how squeamish she is of such rodents, a previous visit having witnessed her standing on a dining-room chair when Gizzy brought in a live mouse. The bravery of expediency. Thank you, Sue G.

The first days at home I did struggle with fitting the stoma, though I only asked one observer to comment, as he arrived as I finished applying a fresh, post-shower bag. He said it was fine despite a big crease down one side, which wasn't *fine* and would leak. Oh yes Kim, did you know one of your girls is a boy?

Would leak ... two words that had a completely

different meaning and context when home from hospital. Little did I know how the leaks, which invariably were large and dam busting, would run my life for the next eight months. Thank goodness I didn't.

As for Evelyn, she was more interested in observing Gizzy than me when I told her that Karen had made my tea. On occasion my anaesthetised mind would manage to recall the observer's name if they were repeat observers …

On the third day, oh joy, the creased Kim was my observer. The stroppy me did not let her indoors for the morning visit. I stood at the front door and said, 'As you can observe I am up. See you at lunchtime.' You just needed to bark back.

Tony was with me during her lunch visit. I informed her that Tony had made my lunch. She then lied about having inspected the house on her initial visit except for the bathroom, which for reasons best known to herself she then needed to observe its layout. Go figure.

The physio, Alex, turned up a bit later that same afternoon. He decided that I needed a course of exercises to strengthen my knees. Advising me that Kim and her team (not girls then) reported into him, he broached the subject of reducing the frequency of the observational visits.

A pattern, of sorts then followed. The morning observer arrived sometime between 10 and 11:30 and left; unless it was Chris, who did the three obs. - of blood pressure, temperature and blood oxygen level.

Then the lunchtime observer turned up between 2 and 4 and got me to do my exercises. Two of which were ridiculously easy, whilst I would have quite liked some arm exercises ... physio Alex however was deaf to this particular post-hospital stay plea. Sadly, poor Alex was off sick when I attempted to make contact and subsequently was taken off my case. Or I was taken off of his!

Observer Kelly wanted the morning visit and lunchtime (i.e. exercise) visit merged into one. I resisted, for now. Kim had already stopped the evening visit from the moment she observed that I had managed to make my supper with neither Karen's nor Tony's assistance.

Questions from the floor?

What if you couldn't answer the door? What if you weren't dressed. Weren't fed? What if …

A few days after my hospital release it was like Piccadilly Circus in my hallway. At the time I was still able to do online shopping for my friend Ed, a service I had started during 2020 once allotted a priority online shop slot, he arrived to collect his portion of the grocery delivery whilst my morning observer was here observing, coincidentally at the same time, it must be stated the one and only time that I had a home visit from a stoma nurse, Stoma Nurse A was part of that morning's circus. The latter, like the male observer had done, commended me on my fresh bag application … the dreaded commendation curse continued to strike for it leaked later on during that day, once the domestic traffic had dissipated.

Early days and keep a food diary were both oft repeated, the latter particularly by the medical profession. So, I duly did.

To me *early days*, however much I reined myself in started to grate. I expected the stoma days to last for one hundred and eighty days … so when did early end? Patience is a virtue, allegedly and

Neil does have it, honest, but not when being patronised with days, weeks and months all being classed as early days. My own kidology of one hundred and eighty days was insufferable enough.

As for the food diary, well that became as much of a joke as the referral to a dietician. Two facts. In all the time I kept a diary it was looked at twice, both somewhat briefly, the first time with no comment whatsoever. I took the diary on a USB stick to my pay-as-you-go April 2022 (!!!!) appointment with my surgeon but Mary-Jane was not allowed to open a third-party file on her computer, so I then emailed the word document to her private secretary. Silence. The second viewing occurred when I had a home visit from a dietician in the employ of Bromley Healthcare … in November 2022, at my request, that is pestering my GP. Though even here Ola was only interested in the last couple of days' eating habits. Four chocolates being lost in translation as four bars of chocolate … as opposed to four individual chocolates. Ho-hum!

The psychological effect of *keep a food diary* being barked at me and appearing as a medical recommendation in print no less, irrespective of me shouting I AM BUT NO-ONE IS FUCKING INTERESTED ENOUGH TO READ IT to myself, was unhealthy. I did state, without the expletive, the above when the food diary suggestion was reiterated to me face-to-face. All to absolutely no avail, which became almost the driving force to the extreme accuracy of the food diary I kept. It is interesting for me now to look back at my different but similar points of focus on the two separate spells of the food diary writing. But that's for later folks, don't want to spoil the plot do we ...

*

Talking of plot, talking loosely ... of a loose plot. Pot. Loos. Nels, stop it!

Okay, initially I used my call button if I suspected my stoma bag was anywhere close to bursting full ... on the whole, the nursing staff appeared to appreciate this. Sometimes, however, they pointed out the ballooning was caused by wind, or even my imagination as I felt the flow of the latest meal exit my body. At times a sci-fi ticklish experience ... not necessarily on my recommended things to try before you die.

Stoma in a teacup

However much the stoma nurses proclaimed that I would be able to cope with the manual dexterity of stoma bag emptying I realised that I needed to find my own solution, preferably, no absolutely before being discharged, thinking of my bathroom as opposed to either lying in a hospital bed or using one of their toilet facilities. I had initially imagined unleashing the detritus into the wash handbasin straight from the stoma bag. Just initially. Apart from splash back this would only really work if the content was purely liquid. Did I really want my shit lingering within the wash handbasin pipework. That is rhetorical, thus no question mark. In hospital I used the *top hats*, that is the papier-mâché vessels that look like inverse top hats used to collect vomit, to drain my bag's contents into. And I had an Einstein brain-switch click. I could use a plastic litre jug as my *top hat*. Freeing both hands to discharge my bag into the jug and then flush the contents down the loo, as well as any subsequent tap water used to clean the jug. Simple. As well as my initial ready-made meals Sue G purchased my first such jug, and I subsequently bought the spare when Tony took me on my first post-op shopping expedition.

Simple, eh? Except when the liquid is a flood

and continuous and over a litre in volume … joy. Indeed, fun for later Nels.

*

The 24th of October, I had been back home less than a week and I hit the panic button!

I was in physical agony with stomach cramps. Nothing was coming out of the stoma opening. Was there a fresh blockage despite the removal of thirty centimetres of my gut? My mind was earning huge overtime payments as it ran rings around calamitous scenarios. What gives?

By 9PM I could not handle my mental isolation, so I telephoned Tony. *What should I do?* The upshot, for which I shall always be grateful, was that he and Sue G drove over from Brentwood and stayed with me till after eight in the morning; by which time the cramps had subsided, discharge had once again started to enter the stoma bag and I had even produced a couple of rock-hard nuggets of jet-black faeces from my anus.

Sweet! Hardly, though plenty of sweat.

Stoma in a teacup

How to describe the agony though, for once it dissipates, I always feel a fraud. But that is me, and not wanting to be a bother. Though I was obviously shit-scared, otherwise I wouldn't even have considered phoning Tony, let things take their course, the trouble being that so close to the op I didn't know what to expect. What exactly was the course to be, this time. The dreaded unknown. Especially when the unknown was exactly what I had gone into hospital with twenty days earlier. Déjà vu! NO!

So, I lie in a foetal position, of sorts, not quite as compact, but my legs are drawn-up towards my stomach. And it is torture, for you are, despite yourself, waiting for the next slap … the build up to the next tightening inside as air bubbles push and shove for space that is not there. It sounds and reads as nothing, something so minor – man-up! Trust me I have; I have sat through plays at the theatre and football matches and held dinner parties doubled-up in agony.

But there is agony and agony and age. Perhaps age takes the biggest toll, as it creeps in almost unbeknownst until someone mentions it, or you accidentally look in the mirror.

And as each bolt of pain stabs as it strikes you tell yourself it is one closer to the end of this particular bout. Except this evening it was so unexpected. Early days or not, I thought that the operation had resolved the issue of the stomach cramps. Thus, my panic, but also refusal to go to A&E, give me a break I had only just come out of hospital. Did that mean that the pain wasn't that bad? No. But I was not having breathing issues this evening, just the all too familiar gut strictures.

Tony and Sue G were very patient with me. And I do know that I am not an ideal patient, except perhaps when laid so low as that night and morning. Previously, once such attacks peak I either pass out or fall asleep.

Sleep!

I just wanted to sleep. I just wanted to feel better. Was I really asking for too much? Help!

It wasn't a question per se of being on my own at night, for after Karen saw me through the first three of those first five days, I was genuinely okay with that it was more the unknown; or worse, a return of the known stomach cramps of

Stoma in a teacup

trapped wind which I thought the *life-saving* operation had resolved.

Early days! How I came to hate hearing those two words being said out loud, even, or especially by me. Especially when I started to say it as a pre-empt. Argh! Seriously, how long were these early days to last?

It transpired, more by default than design, that so far as the medical profession was concerned three months after the operation were the *early days*. Half-way to the six months and the stoma reversal.

Oh, those early days of believing that come the 6th of April, 2022, I would be operated on and wake up without a stoma and life would return to …

In these COVID-19 years what would life return to? Early days …

And I was taking baby steps, and there was a learning curve. The observer visits were already down to two per day. The evening visit had lasted three evenings. As stated on the final one of the day Kim herself had observed me

111

managing to feed myself. Tick!

*

The days that followed the hiatus of the *early days weekend* were not clever, in a health sense. I was feeling somewhat fey, Tony was back over from Brentwood, basically a weekly visit at this stage of my recuperation, and a somewhat more thorough observation than that of those whose job it was, and he was concerned, which transmitted itself to me (super receptive as I was) and via phone calls the on duty stoma nurse became concerned, and eventually advised on the Thursday of the week in question that doctors would see me right away in the Surgical Ambulatory Unit if I arrived within an hour. Could I get there now? Now? Yes, as now as possible, before 4PM. They would give me a quick MOT, on this, the last Thursday of October.

Sue H, theatre-going friend, was due to visit and offered to be my chauffeur, should they decide to keep me in, and straight down to the PRUH we went, arriving just before the 4PM mark ... dropping me off before going to sort out parking. By the time she came back to see how I was getting along they had decided to keep me in overnight, all night on a trolley not a bed.

A trolley with a pillow but no pillow case, the hospital had run out ... (if I was allowed supper should I try for a baked potato!) ... and I was put on a rehydration drip ... twenty-four hours later, Friday afternoon, a bed within a ward was found ... my old ward. One more night's stay kept being added till release on the Monday ... by which time the calendar had clicked its October cogs and become November.

I spent a night of diminished sleep on the trolley that Thursday night. (My final to date experience of the ASU was thirteen months later and they had upgraded their trolleys for beds.) A trolley is a very narrow contraption for a night long sleep.

Sleep! You are having a laugh. If only ... destined to be positioned next to the nurses' station and they have their radio on all night. Well ASU patients aren't really ill, are they? They can walk right? Ambulatory.

And Elton sang *I think it's gonna be a long, long time*[2]. Too fucking right, I thought, and laughed

[2] Rocket Man (I think it's going to be a long, long time) – Bernie Taupin

insanely into my towel-covered pillow. I had asked for a towel as without a pillowcase the surface of the bare pillow was made of a slippery synthetic fabric that refused to stay in situ. Such a fuss pot.

During a night of marginal shut-eye I first laid eyes on Laura of Arabia and her rushing about like a headless chicken as if she had failed to deliver the next instalment of the Arabian Nights and had been beheaded for her pains. If only, would have saved me a whole load of pains two months on.

But no, she darted about, clomp-clomping in inappropriate footwear as well as attire. But what did I know, a dehydrated ambulatory insomniac with attitude. It is interesting how unobserved you are if you lie still on your trolley. Clomp-clomp. Still but awake, for such a long, long time. Her claim for infamy within these pages to be revealed at the turn of the year …

Morning! At this point in its location within the PRUH the ASU had its own drinks' station, as well as a disproportionate staff to patient ratio compared to the wards. Coffee, tea, biscuit – on demand. I had to smile, between shits.

The passing Mary-Jane, my surgeon's rounds obviously included those trolley-bound on ASU, and entourage decided that I should be kept in and transferred to a ward. Friday morning and the weekend starts here.

It seemed like but minutes since I had escaped from the clutches of Surgical Ward 8, but here I was back. But the but was big. I was back as a different person mentally. The anaesthetic fog lifted, at last ... and I could read again. The joy, the sheer joy of being able to concentrate enough to read. The rights to this huge moment in my recovery fell to Madeline Miller's *The Song of Achilles*. My previous inability to focus meant I had but brought the one book in with me. And even with trying to space out my gobbling up its pages I had finished the delightful novel by the Sunday morning.

HELP! I screamed, but in a positive way. Thank goodness Sarah had promised to visit later that afternoon. My WhatsApp response to her *Can I bring anything?* one, was pen, paper and chocolate – or words that included those three, no doubt including both a please and a thank you.

Sarah delivered and I actually started writing this tome in hospital on October 31st 2021, recalling my first encounter with *the observers*. That still makes me laugh.

Assuming all comedy is black, even if just at the edges, I think the funniest moment in a spontaneous sense occurred on the Saturday of that weekend back in hospital. It was one of those had-to-be-there moments. I was not laughing at the patient, despite what may seem like a somewhat callous action on my part. You had to be there ...

A *fresh* in-bed patient was being wheeled into the recently vacated bay opposite me. Man was he moaning. Bloody hell, thought my kind self; then the selfish me kicked in, how is the newly zoomed into focus me supposed to concentrate with that racket going on. *Ha-ah-ah-ah!* Cried the new arrival. *Ha-ah-ah-ah*, on a regular rhythmic, repeat cycle. As the rear porter pushed the emptied of its contents transfer bed out of the side ward in perfect timing to the patient's ha-ah-ah-ah he thrust his right arm in the air à la John Travolta dancing to *Stayin' alive* and grinned at me. Sheer unadulterated wickedness. I

Stoma in a teacup

returned the grin, and how. As I keep saying, you had to be there. But as you weren't my wicked bone recorded my fellow inmate's *ha-ah-ah-ah* and forwarded it via WhatsApp accompanied by the description of the porter's moves. No shame. Apologies.

Though, in fact it should be the hospital apologising to him. Compensating him. His angst and level of yelps got worse, increasing in volume as well as losing their rhythm. Sorry mate! Goodness knows how long his cries went on for, it must have seemed like an eternity for him. From my vantage point it appeared as if every member of the nursing staff had tried to ascertain what was wrong with him, other than the fact that he was not passing any urine through his catheter. There's always one, isn't there … thank goodness … a doctor who discovered that the poor man's catheter had been inserted incorrectly. Ouch, times, and times again. OUCH!

My point here is culpability. In my line of work there was no blame culture but the fault's source would be uncovered and dealt with, rectified so that it should not recur. Here the doctor just barked a fix-it to the ward staff, obviously an appropriate command in itself, without dealing with the root cause, for it had occurred in the operating theatre. How would the person who had done the botched job, whilst I must add, the patient was under the influence of an anaesthetic, learn if no-one told them?

As for the *ouch* levels? They reached new heights, almost bringing tears to my own eyes as the nursing staff extracted the inaccurately placed catheter tube, only to reinsert it correctly. The poor man. Having experienced catheter insertion when not under an anaesthetic my sympathies were one hundred percent with the fellow. The pain trauma, even as relief at finally being able to have pee course through his body, must have been excruciating. He wasn't well in the first place. Right?

Stayin' alive!

And as for this patient, well since Thursday's walk-in admission my prescribed loperamide intake per day had doubled, having gone from eight at the time of admission to twelve it was now sixteen, to try and thicken up my stoma discharge. As I WhatsApp messaged both Karen and Tony, complete trial and error. The

Stoma in a teacup

professionals did not actually know. And all I could ascertain was that I would not be allowed home without a significant thickening of my stoma output. Sixteen appeared to be working with hopefully hospital discharge a by-product of this less fluid consistency. The only return to liquid occurred after downing a flagon of *build-you-up* Fortisip ... the staff nurse and I agreed we would overlook this blip. The stoma nurse who visited me on the Monday morning once again advised that I was doing a splendid job in affixing my stoma bag, and that it was down to me to adjust my loperamide input as required. Compliments were still going hand in hand with leakages ...

The advice of a dietician might be useful.

Talking of loperamide input, the stoma nurses always recommended that I take my loperamide immediately before meals, which made perfect sense. But they then shrugged their collective shoulders when I mentioned that meal times and medication dispensing times did not sync whilst inhabiting a hospital ward. Yet the Fortisip drinks tended to be distributed at meal times. Go figure! Also, the hospital ward loperamide were in tablet form unlike the instant melts that the hospital dispensed in my discharge pack, the latter type was also the kind that were prescribed for collection at my pharmacy of choice throughout my stoma days. The early ones and beyond.

I was discharged early in the afternoon of the first Monday in November.

It's not what you know but who you know. As it happens pre-ASU visit and subsequent hospital stay my first COVID-19 booster vaccine had been booked for later that afternoon, at the Ramsden estate pharmacy. As I walked into the PRUH's departure lounge I bumped into Kath Buckley, a friend of a friend, who was volunteering at the hospital in the vaccine department. To cut to the quick, Kath fixed it for me to be vaccinated then and there. Thank you. Tick, done. Therefore, Tony did not need to drive me around the borough, it was straight home to Gizzy.

Okay, now to stay out of hospital, take two. And now only four weeks until my scheduled, okay anticipated, follow-up consultation with Mary-Jane. Onwards and upwards. Games, kidology, whatever gets you through the day.

November 2021

Released again from hospital I started the *Stoma Diaries*. Now pasting the first days' entries into *Stoma in a teacup* my diligence amazes me, for by the end, when it was obvious, despite all telling me to keep a food diary that no-one was ever going to read the bloody thing, it became almost nothing but a record of my loperamide intake, my meals and stoma outages.

A sample of the obedient if naïve patient ...

<u>NOVEMBER</u>

<u>2/11</u>

First full day home – 16 Imodium

spaced throughout day – from 07:30 to 22:00. Basically nothing much but wind and some sticky black discharge till around 20:00. After which about 1 litre of murky liquid.

Food - two slices of white bread with shredless shred marmalade; two slices of buttered white bread with prawns; mashed banana with sugar; salmon fillet with mashed potato; Alpro dessert; bag of jelly babies; some rich tea biscuits during course of day; six chocolate buttons.

3/11

Not much in bag upon wake-up, black and slightly less liquid. 1st 4 Imodium at 08:00. Breakfast of two slices of white bread with shredless shred marmalade. Six fingers of shortbread.

2nd 4 Imodium at 12:35, lunch consisted of two slices of buttered white bread with prawns; mashed banana with sugar. A few shortbread fingers during afternoon. Don't think I drank enough as felt faint upon standing for a longer period than normal.

3rd 4 Imodium at 17:37, supper cooked chicken breast and penne; homemade rice pudding.

First emptying of bag. Dark thick treacle, but still liquid as opposed to solid.

4th 4 Imodium at 22:08. Yorkie bar and some rich tea biscuits. Bag contents emptied pre-bed, as above, perhaps a tad more viscous. That is the least I have emptied a bag since having a stoma.

4/11

1st 4 Imodium at 06:36, emptied bag – gravy, almost runny. Breakfast of two slices of white bread with shredless shred marmalade.

2nd 4 Imodium at 11:36, goats' cheese on two slices of white bread, half a roast beef sandwich also on white bread. Couple of rich tea biscuits. Stoma contents thicker, smellier. More wind that the last couple of days.

3rd 4 Imodium at 17:56, chicken, bacon, potato and cheese topped bake, followed by homemade rice pudding. More wind and thicker smellier poo. Fudge pieces and chocolate buttons.

4th 4 Imodium at 21:55.
… but as the days turned to weeks and then, alarmingly to months, my entries more often than not were scaled back to the bare four lines of when I took my instant Imodium melts and the day's three meals. Yes, I would annotate with stomach cramps and particularly eventful stoma bag outages. All done with a growing perversity as who was actually going to read about my forthcoming marshmallow and jelly baby intake? Referencing early days advice from the stoma nurses …

> *'In terms of the loperamide, I would say why don't you first try to alter your diet as there are things that can help thicken the stoma output naturally.*
>
> *Have you tried having things like jelly babies/marshmallows? Or increasing the amounts of starchy foods you are having like pasta/potatoes/white bread/salty crips?'*

I should have been reading the signs that they were clueless already, but I wasn't for what did I know, though perhaps there is an edge of frustration as well as sarcasm already creeping into my reply …

> FYI I have white bread for breakfasts and lunches and potato or pasta with every evening meal. Will go and get myself salty crisps, jelly babies and marshmallows this afternoon – pleased that I like them all.

*

My hospital discharge letter advised that I would be seen by my surgeon or one of the team in six weeks.

One of the lowest points after the ileostomy trauma itself, was hearing from the stoma nurses, who I had asked to chase up on the issue on my behalf, was that my first post-op appointment with Mary-Jane was to be on January the 14th. A confirmation letter would shortly be in the post. January the 14th, over three months after the initial operation! Over halfway to the six months before I could expect a reversal operation to occur.

The latter thought should have been a positive, as friends tried to advise me it was, but to me it already appeared as timelapse slippage, and I was still reasonably upbeat. I had regained my ability to read. Alcohol was about to reappear on the menu and I would soon be behind the steering wheel of my car again. Though the latter decision was now mine to make, for I had assumed questions like driving, resumption of tennis, going on holiday etc., would be answered during the first post-op consultation. Think again! It would all depend on how I felt. I invested in seatbelt clips that allowed a looser seatbelt fitting across one's midriff – so as not to squash my stoma whilst driving, though using four plastic food-bag air locking clips worked better. They stayed locked; it turned out that the purpose designed seatbelt one had to be readjusted on each drive. My fingers were not impressed, so I reverted to my Heath Robinson solution.

*

Note to self - Half an hour since your latest four Imodium, best go and have your white bread sandwich. Yummy!

Yes folks, as random as it reads.

*

Talking of STUPID, I entertained the Sunday Club[3] to super on the Saturday following my latest hospital discharge ... as per my diet sheet ... and with a glass of white, via the telephone and within Tony's hearing, I asked the stoma nurse on Thursday 4th November whether I could imbibe and she said yes. I imbibed with a lot of

---

[3] Sunday Club – during the glorious Covid-19 summer of 2020 Ed, Sue H and Doreen would partake in Sunday afternoon intercourse in my garden within the social distancing guidelines.

caution; no way did I want the week's progress lost.

There were extenuating factors to my foolhardiness in entertaining my friends, other than Neil trying to prove something to himself, Ed was not well and this meal needed hosting now. As it turned out Ed was at the beginning of his own protracted descent into the hell of ill health with throat cancer and for what would seem like forever; this Saturday was the one day when my diet and his ability to swallow merged for months to come.

*

I assumed the fact that there was, to my mind, nowhere else to turn, was why I emailed the likes of *thanks again for your support* at the end of my November emails to the stoma nurses. I even sent them a *thank you* card (one of my African photocards). Retrospectively I would beg the question *thanks for what*, telling me that they had never before come across someone with my issues.

Apologies. My fault. Excuse my existence why don't you. But way too early for any of that.

Dear Karen had tried levity with *let's name it*. I couldn't be arsed, sorry Karen. So let her choose Julian. It stuck.

I was still trying to deal with the day-to-day reality of having this stoma bag attachment as well as the practicalities of ordering my stoma related supplies.

If in doubt, sorry stoma nurses, but it was back to you …

> When you say *regular order with Fittleworth* what do you mean, what does that include? I ordered wipes, for the red soreness around the stoma on Monday, and then some hygienic wipes on Wednesday – well I think I did – I received email acknowledgements though have yet to receive anything. Does this mean that my order is on hold – *This was the email acknowledgement … 'Your order will be dispatched in accordance with your existing delivery cycle and General Practitioners (GP's) instructions.*

> *Please allow between 2 to 10 days accordingly as we will dispatch your goods upon receipt of your prescription'.* As I have no wipes are they waiting for a cyclical delivery?

So, in the early days the stoma nurses would leave emergency supplies at the PRUH reception desk. I soon realised that this process was not similar to doing my Sainsbury's shop online, and that forward planning was very much essential to a smooth supply chain and removing one of the stressful points of this coming to terms business.

By the middle of November my diet of mashed potato, white bread and pasta was sort of doing my head in, even with the adding of salty crisps, jelly babies and marshmallows. In fact, I nearly puked up marshmallows having consumed a whole bag. Piggy! On this occasion they did seem to thicken my stoma bag output. On this occasion …

My head was still dealing with the fact that Mary-Jane would not be seeing me until the 14th of January. Two months away.

Stoma in a teacup

There had to be some sort of release for this frustration, so I wrote …

It is six weeks today since you operated on me. Whilst in hospital I was told that my follow up appointment would be six weeks from then. Today I received a letter from the appointments' officer, dated 10th November, advising me that you (or a member of your team) will not be seeing me until 14thJanuary, 2022! Is this correct? Am I really to have no medical support or review for a further two months?

Is my sole point of recourse the stoma nurse team? (Who by the way also expected my follow up appointment to be six weeks after the operation.)

Who is to advise on when I am fit to drive? When I can resume any degree of physical activity? Theatre attendance? Travel and holidays? Are these decisions mine to take depending on how I feel on the day?

I do appreciate that some of the

> above would appear minor issues but they are not for the individual concerned.
>
> Is the delay in an outpatient appointment an indication that reversal of the stoma will not after all take place on or around 6th April, 2022?
>
> Yours,
>
> cc Stoma nurses

Obviously, a void swallowed it in one gulp. Radio silence only went to increase where I shouldn't have been mentally, it was difficult to avoid feeling cast adrift …

*

By default, of having the stoma bag, awareness of my bodily functions appeared heightened. More so those that had now disappeared from my life. Mid-month my *Stoma Diaries* state that *I let out wind and felt that I needed to go to toilet, though nothing came out*. Wind release one of the functions that had disappeared, I assumed, with the bag's intervention in the chain of descent. I used to be ace at letting out wind, mostly … well actually perhaps not that mostly at

Stoma in a teacup

all … as wasn't it trapped wind that had got me in this fine pickle anyway. Yes, okay Neil. But that's not the point. The point is, and there is one, is that how come I was expediting wind as well as feeling the urge to poo. Was this similar to a foot-amputee still being able to feel his toes?

The stoma nurses advised that there was residual poo that would work its way out. They hadn't mentioned residual wind. Residual wind? And I have an urge to be oh so flippant. Retrospective flippancy is allowed, isn't it? Flippancy was the last thing on my mind barely a month after the op; my first social outing had just occurred – to Orpington's Pato Lounge courtesy of Peter-the-train taking me to my podiatry appointment and me treating us to a coffee and a tea-cake.

But now *residual wind* sounds like either the name of a pop group or the dying gusts from a storm. Yet, it seems, that I must possess residual wind. And after the tea-cake instant poo. Oh Julian!

It wasn't just residual wind I possessed, and over the coming weeks I would, via the internet learn how to deal with it as I sadly learnt that the stoma nurses knew what they knew as opposed to what was new.

The 4th of November or a month-after-two-days-before and I was still learning. The discharge was burning my skin, how I needed those wipes that had yet to appear from Fittleworth. I tried to adjust the position that I affixed the bag, not that there was yet that much room to manoeuvre. Wriggle room there was not. Was there a correspondence between keeping my liquid intake up with the extent of the liquid output I discharged? I know I did not want readmittance to the PRUH and had added a bottle of Lucozade Sport, with half a teaspoonful of salt, to my daily hydration routine; as well as two white wine glasses of wine of any hue. Maintaining sanity by dint of alcohol use.

*

Perforce, as there was to be no guidance on when I should resume driving the decision was mine to make. Decided to think positively about this, therefore will start driving etc. when I feel fit enough if there is to be no medical guidance.

I had been back driving for a couple of weeks

before I ventured as far afield as to watch the mighty Crystal Palace play Aston Villa, a three o'clock kick-off on a Saturday afternoon – honest!

The mighty Palace lost. I was gutted on many fronts. I have never been a Steven Gerard fan for the most awful of initial reasons … his voice. The second reason is that he successfully managed Glasgow Rangers … boo! Then the fact that he dropped them and joined Villa when they unceremoniously sacked Dean Smith earlier that November. Money, money, money with no long-term memory or long-term loyalty. I had not been keen on Villa, sorry Prince William, from back in the Roy Ellis days as chairman. Yes, that far back, refocuses your mind, and mine, on how old I actually am. Anyway, Ellis's return resulting in Ron Saunders departure, fresh from having won the league title. Loyalty and reward … bye-bye. I have always been careful not to wish relegation on any team, the superstition of it coming back to bite your own team. Roy Ellis's behaviour towards the plethora of managers he shredded made it a close call.

Regardless, Villa beat Palace and Stevie G was the new hero. Short-lived as ever at Villa, with or without Ellis.

Back to myself and I was pleased at how the body and stoma had behaved. When I had advised my friends, my own band of supporters, of my decision to go to the game I had also stated as a caveat for me as well as their peace of mind that I would take each stage at a time; the departure, the drive, the walk, half-time. Progress to the next step dependent on the successful completion of the preceding one. Basically, how I felt. Though knowing myself full well once I set off for the match I would only be returning once the job was done.

All went well. Job done. Almost. But almost is not good enough.

Fuck no!

Two roads away from home I suddenly felt a chill around my midriff. With one hand on the steering wheel the other explored below the layers of clothing ... saturated. Once garage parked, I discovered the full extent of the stoma bag disaster. My first experience of litres of liquid emanating from my middle. Other than my boots, scarf and bobble hat beanie everything else I had been clothed in went straight into the washing machine. Even my socks, as they got contaminated in my undressing.

The entry in my *Stoma Diaries* reads - *From knees to nipples soaking wet in poo.*

After personal cleansing there was the car seat to attend to. My first action was to soak up as best as possible, using sheets and sheets and more sheets of kitchen towel, the lingering dampness that had escaped beyond my clothing into the fabric of the car seat. Man did that eat up kitchen towel paper. The next job, that is when I thought the return from trying to extract further shit from the seat was a tad futile, was to use a fabric cleaner. Again, as best as one could.

Brightside-Andrews was delighted that the discharge tsunami had been by and large a clear liquid one and in shit smelling terms whilst not pleasant it could have been so much worse. (Obviously thick regular faeces would not have spread so far and wide and silently. But hey-ho!)

I was eventually satisfied that I had cleaned the upholstery as much as possible without getting it done professionally. *Hi yes, can you clean the driver's side seat please. It's full of shit.*

What I did for some weeks after was sit on my boot liner under which I had placed fresh kitchen towel until there was no dampness left on said paper at journey's end. Even after reassured that the car seat was now dry, I sat on the boot liner just in case of future accidents whilst out and about.

As this happened at the end of November I was concerned about mildew and how would the seat dry off as well as any residual smell that the next passengers would have to deal with. It did dry, and there was thankfully no comment on any odour. Perhaps passengers thought it was just part and parcel of me and my stoma, but I don't think so.

The close of a particularly interesting chapter. Thankfully a one-off or the stoma-bag-attached me would have stopped attending football.

*

In re-reading my food intake diaries of this period I note the pains I was having in the small of my back. Pains that were severe enough for even me to have to take paracetamol tablets, as the pain as opposed to stoma leakages was waking me up during the course of the night.

Whatever it was was thankfully short lived. Severe enough for me to be concerned and make note of it at the time though, from 26th November through to 4th December. Causing me to wake between two and three in the morning and force myself to sleep on beyond six. My diary wondered if it was related to weight loss, and was a kidney issue. Yet from 5th December there is no further mention of it, and I do recall its non-recurrence as opposed to its disappearance, as such. Waking for a wee during the subsequent nights and not having the pain as opposed to being woken up with the pain kicking in was a relief. And I gladly grabbed at any positives that meant this body wasn't completely crumbling like a dunked digestive.

*

You can revisit. Oh, and I do. I have a season ticket, it's as though it's my favourite National Trust or RHS garden, I need to be within its walls. But in reality, even mine, it's a prison, admittedly of my own making. Life without. Solitary.

So how? How did we get here? I laugh, of course, for it is only myself here.

And it doesn't take two. It was all my own doing.

Should I have sought psychotherapy? Should I seek psychotherapy, even at this late stage? Help other than my own *deal with it* stance. Was my single status a mental issue? Emotional walls that allowed no scaling? Financial walls via imbued or misconstrued parental concerns? A sexuality that cannot reconcile itself to its physicality?

Is falling for the wrong people a defence mechanism? In search of unrequited love? Or is that really too perverse?

What I do know is that tomorrow's answers would be different from today's.

December 2021

I don't know how, perhaps my almost tearful voice, with tears momentarily attached, helped, but the stoma nurses arranged for me to have blood tests at the PRUH on December the 2nd. I must have cited the back pains as well as my concerns over my weight loss and the fact that four times four loperamide a day, even with marshmallows and jelly babies, was not stopping the discharging of my intake with it seemingly barely touching the sides. What goodness was being absorbed? It now of course, had half the distance to run, so to speak!

The blood test results were more a psychological blow than the positive of the physical well-being they reported; for, if this was me well, then what was I going to have to put up with until the stoma reversal. And if that occurred on the 6th of April, I still had four months of this faecal mess to plough through. Joy!

*

7/12
1st 4 Imodium at 06:57, cornflakes and stewed apple.

2nd 4 Imodium at 12:10, fish pie, rice krispie marshmallow square.

3rd 4 Imodium at 19:10, cheese and ham panini and chips.

What a mess. UNDERSTATEMENT! I can't have a pint of beer with a stoma, and the marshmallows were useless.

4th 4 Imodium at 22:20, two slices of white bread with shredless shred marmalade.

The above extract from my *keep-a-food-diary* food diary, other than being fairly representative of my diet is also a witness to my one and only pint of beer whilst sporting the stoma bag accoutrement. I thought Karen had said that the real-life Julian was a lager drinker! Nels! The occasion, my first post hospital release venture to the Tuesday social gathering of local gays that *Miss* Jones chairs at the Sovereign of the Seas. Thankfully, oh yes, there's always cause to be thankful however awful the experience, and it's true, it can always be worse. As I was saying, thankfully I realised almost immediately after its consumption that a pint of beer and a stoma do not go together. Whereas I would have expected the pint to want to exit my body via my urinary tract, NO – it was finding the stoma a more direct route to adios my body.

As my bag began swelling, I beat a hasty retreat for home and my bathroom sink, that is my wash-hand-basin, and where my plastic litre jug sat in anticipation. More than a pint exited into the container and surrounds, it was as if the pint had triggered a release valve, except I no longer had said valve – it had been removed as part of the thirty centimetres that was no more after the ileostomy. Which was another piece of medical info deposited into a conversation by a stoma nurse as opposed to pre-discharge *pay attention* facts. But as ever, a bathroom clean-up followed by a rejuvenating shower, the attaching of a new stoma bag and I felt clean, warm and cosy and ready for two slices of white bread spread with butter and marmalade-without-bits preceded by my last loperamide of the day. The human condition? The Neil Andrews condition.

*

Also obvious at the beginning of December was that the stoma was shrinking enough for me to have the conversation with the stoma nurses about the size of the bag aperture. The better the fit the less skin irritation from the discharge as well as less wriggle space for the discharge to seep out – allegedly.

I saw the nurses, who initially cut a number of bags with a 50 mm opening, and that's the size I requested from my supplier when I re-ordered. My stoma supply orders were copied to my doctor's surgery for approval, and I believe were also copied to the stoma nurses, for information, I suppose.

I raised the issue of the liquidity of my discharge in my chat with the stoma nurse, again the response was that the loperamide dosage was down to the patient. Great! Thanks!

I was following the strictures of the recommended diet, falling seriously out of love with marshmallows and jelly babies!

Oh well, whatever, heal yourself, so here goes … from the 13th December I topped my loperamide dosage up from sixteen a day to twenty a day. What possible harm could it do? Anything for a thicker discharge.

A strange wish really, for the more liquid the discharge the easier the decanting and flushing away. But it wasn't right … the substance of my discharge that is.

What also wasn't right was the fact that my discharge letter stated the following: *Follow up that we have arranged – Mary-Jane's clinic in 4 to 6 weeks.* Right! Yes, oh yes, it still rankled, however much I told myself that calm was the only way forward. Please do take as read the expletives I refuse, in this instance, to type.

So, twenty loperamide a day as we enter the festive season. The seasonal jollifications again decimated by COVID-19 restrictions. For sure I did not want to catch COVID-19 but it was relatively a secondary consideration to my quest which remained an uninterrupted forty-eight-hour stoma bag wearing experience. The bag being changed after every other day's shower.

Was that really too much to ask for for Christmas. No question mark, rhetorical.

And yet another thing, it was at this time of increasing my loperamide dosage that I noticed that the pharmacist short changed the NHS by at least eight tablets per prescription. I wondered what the pharmacy was invoicing for?

Another *Stoma Diaries* extract …

> 20/12/21
>
> Still having leakage issues with the bags at night, due I think to weight loss/body shape.
> Particularly bad for me last night as ended up having to wash my bathroom floor at 2:30 in the morning! (Thankfully that's the

first time I have had such an
extreme accident.)

*

Dream on! Hold on, is it really that much to ask?

Dear Father Christmas …

*

Though, as stated elsewhere, my toes are my
Achilles' heel my fingers are a close second, but
from a different standpoint. My mother would
have said sheer clumsiness along the lines of *I
knew that was going to happen*, whereupon,
either under my breath or by mere thought retort
within *in which case why let it*! I know I have let
the pre-plastic bank notes slip through my fingers
before now, only realising once some way from
the likely scene; the breakages of crockery
manifold, thankfully mostly here as opposed to
here, there and everywhere. The latter invoking
trepidation on the part of both guest and host.
Can he manage? As if I am not there.

Then there's by extension my nightmare disaster
scenario syndrome. If I park near or walk by a

street drain cover, I tighten my grip on my keys, or pat my pocket to make sure that they are secure and cannot jump out and disappear down the culvert. It's never happened, touch wood, and don't rightly know why or how the fear started. The drain slats do seem excessively wide. Mind the gap.

And exiting trains has become a post-stoma issue … even with a crutch my left knee has chosen to collapse under me on two separate occasions as I have taken the step off the train at Orpington station. On the second occasion my crutch slipped between the train and the platform and I had to await the arrival of a special retrieval team. So, so embarrassing for the man I used to be.

*

An all too brief interlude, and the result of theatre bookings made as COVID and safe distancing still ruled our way of living our lives, but an excursion. Well, I am truly blessed, like you didn't know this already, otherwise please explain to me how I managed an unscathed excursion to the theatre with but the one during-performance stoma burp, which Sue H kindly says she didn't hear, unlike the two mobile phones which we did all too loud and clear ... So yes, after the weekend of endless bag changes what was the chance of that happening? If only I was a betting man! Back to *normal* today, black treacle everywhere, on my fourth bag as I type. If cleanliness is next to Godliness, then by Jove I am right there, as close as one can get.

*

In a way Neil-like-on-purpose I purchased and subsequently cooked a whole turkey on Christmas day, supplemented, so as not to turn into a turkey myself, by home cooking from friends Eileen and Jane. But I could neither put on weight nor turn my input into more solid output ... and on the 27th of December was woken up at 03:38 by the stoma bag contents discharging across my torso.

Later that day I started to experience the worse stomach pains since the 23rd of October; if you recall, when I had phoned Tony and he and Sue G had come and stayed with me until eight the next morning.

This is the extract from the diary dated December

28th ...

> Oh, what a night/morning –
> vomiting of white bile –
> excruciating stomach pains.
>
> TWO stoma bag changes – so bad
> I didn't realise the first leak had
> happened, the second after I had
> passed out asleep.

I persevered with the five loperamide four times a day, right up to the year end. Though my discharge remained liquid and excessive as my weight loss continued. I now tipped the scales at under sixty-five kilograms.

January 2022

Happy New Year! 2022 must be better than 2021 etc. Flippancy and how far into 2022 are we …

Actually, for a second let's put the chimes on hold. Sue H and I were unable to say *no* to Doreen's New Year's Eve supper invitation. Why? Well Doreen's year had been even worse than mine, with her bowel cancer and chemotherapy and she also had a stoma to deal with … for the rest of her life. And I should complain? Relative. Trust me. And as for the fourth member of the Sunday Club, Ed, well Ed was in hospital with pneumonia, complications after weeks of radiotherapy to treat his throat cancer had left him weak and susceptible. Sue H the only healthy one amongst us.

Sue H hates New Year. She also hates Christmas. Sometimes I think she hates being healthy.

But we agreed to attend, for an early supper. No staying on for Big Ben. I was not well. I knew I was not well. I was trying not to panic. I felt another blockage in my diminished pipelines of gut. I could not control the sweat, Sue H rightly thought she should get me home.

I was in bed by ten, and cannot recall hearing any celebratory fireworks. I spent the next day in bed, giving in to the pain at 14:43 when I phoned 111. Tony and Sue H had independently advised me to follow this course of action, however much any resultant visit to casualty was anathema to me. Sue H had phoned to see how I was after the Hogmanay meal at Doreen's, whilst I had phoned Tony for advice. Whether I would take it or not was always another matter, but Tony knew this.

152

Hearing nothing from 111 I redialled at 16:20; come early evening neither Tony nor Sue H could believe me when I advised that I still had heard nothing back from 111. The eventual return call was received at 21:22; the advice being to take myself off to A&E for if they called me an on-call doctor he would as likely send me to A&E anyway. So sometime around 10PM I called a friend, one I knew would be sober, diabetic Peter-the-train, asking him to take me to A&E. Thankfully he was both able and willing to oblige, minimising his lugubrious posturing for my benefit. He dropped me off and kindly said I could call him back for a lift home should I be discharged once seen. Once seen I was taken through to what I recognised as the *ambulatory surgical unit*, the night doctor in charge was the same one as on my late October stay, straight from the Fry's Turkish delight advert, in my humble but out dated opinion, the inappropriately dressed Laura of Arabia! I was scanned, and her diagnosis was constipation, to stop the loperamide and take a laxative instead. But they had none on the ward only baked potatoes (I jest. Nels! Okay!), and of course the pharmacy was closed. Not to worry I said, I have some Laxido at home. Sorted. But hey, now you're here, stay the night. Don't mind if I do. Stupid, I know. But little did I know the outcome of her casualness.

On cue, as I was wolfing down a bowl of cornflakes my bag burst. When I advised the assisting nurse how often this happened, he asked why I didn't use banana strips. What? Banana strips? He then went on to explain that they were sealing strips that were used to reinforce the stoma watertightness. Good to know. Thank you, stoma nurses, knowledge is power ... need to know basis ...

Peter called at 07:53 to say he had arrived to take me home. I had to go home in a hospital gown thanks to the latest bag bursting incident having soiled the clothes he had deposited me wearing the night before.

So back home I have my first Laxido sachet at 08:30 after having put the soiled clothes in the wash and showered. Then off to bed, the intent some undisturbed sleep.

For some reason I am still dosing myself with loperamide. I take two at 17:50 after having had to shower again, attaching the third stoma bag of the day to my body. I follow that up at 19:20 with another couple of loperamide, making that four today as opposed to the twenty-a-day I was on over the holidays.

I can only assume that the nonsense of taking both a laxative and a loperamide was due to my state of ill health befuddling my common sense. Or sheer perversity?

The next morning, which was the Bank Holiday of Monday the 3rd, I took another Laxido sachet at 07:41. My food intake was minimal, cornflakes. For some reason I was still following Laura of Arabia's advice, so took another sachet of the laxative at 13:38. Even though things weren't right. How can they have been as I took three loperamide at 17:28, crossing my fingers that the new stoma bag would be watertight.

It was watertight. But that was the least of my worries after one of the worst, if not the worst, night of my life.

It is one thing being seriously ill, as in and out of consciousness, on drugs that are managing the issues that you are experiencing, there but not there so to speak.

This was not like that. I was wide awake with the

most amazing stomach cramps. Not amazing in a good way. I knew there was no point either dialling 111 or asking Peter to take me back to casualty. Hadn't I done what the doctor prescribed? I literally lay in my bed all night waiting for one of the washing-machine like gurgles and spins to be my last, for my guts to rupture. I do not exaggerate. There was no way my innards could survive the next tumult. Would the end be quick, would the current stoma bag fly off. (Difficult to do under the duvet!) I assume, as always with my stomach cramps I eventually passed into some semblance of sleep as the pain abated somewhere around 4AM.

And yes, I did think of the life I have lived. I find it hard to describe what I went through that night. I wish I had recorded my screams. Screams that underlay my fears. Not of dying per se but would it be protracted, was this part of it?

The next morning, a call to the stoma nurses at the PRUH sorted one thing out. Don't take any laxative product if you have a stoma, they couldn't understand why the doctor had said it was the course of treatment for what she diagnosed as constipation.

One thing hadn't changed as I initially returned to eight loperamide a day, bag leakage … note to self that I must remember to ask about banana strips. For sure, any stoma bag with a sense of self was going to leak if all I was discharging into it was dirty liquid!

Yet again Karen came to save the day. Thankfully the room she and Kevin used when stoma-sitting had been prepped by Reggie, the person who did, so I had no need to make an ascent to my home's second storey. I liked to keep my feet on the ground. That's verging on flippancy Nels.

However resilient you may be as a solo individual sometimes you really do need another body to share your living space, even if they can't actually do anything when the stoma's misbehaving, it's a comfort knowing they're there. On a couple of the nights my bag started to leak approaching bedtime, so off I went to change it and shower, whilst Karen headed upstairs for bed. She therefore missed the expletives mixed with crazed laughter as I stood in the shower waiting for the shit to stop pouring out of me. It is really hard to comprehend until it actually happens to you. Thank goodness, how many times have I thanked goodness within these pages? Thank goodness on this occasion I was patient and waited. On occasion I have been known to jump the gun, no disqualification just poo all over the bathroom floor. And yet again that amazing feeling of comfort and cosiness once dry, fresh bag attached and clean PJs on. Weird! Mind over matter? When minutes before it mattered so much, when I was on my hands and knees cleaning my own faeces off of the bathroom floor. And Karen did not hear a thing when I recounted my tale at breakfast. Bless her, for feeling bad, though I had been vocal my voice has never been one that carries. Where needed, I had become adept at using my silence and my look as my own equivalent of being loud. And to be totally honest, cleaning your faeces off your bathroom floor is a private matter, manic laugh ... forgive me Karen!

Now, as if my about-to-breakdown washing-machine stomach wasn't enough of a highlight for the first full week of the year. Obviously not. And to think that Karen missed this too. Lucky Karen! To think, I repeat, that I had had a sensible, recommended even, meal that evening – salmon and penne. My *Stoma Diaries* entry from that evening is accurate but way too black and white for what actually occurred ... *What is the point of the diet – over TWO litres of liquid discharge with penne confetti.* Actually, maybe this is already too much information for some. In which case THEY will have not reached this far. To continue, I was calmly watching television when I suddenly felt that I was perhaps in need of bag emptying. Perhaps! Too late, for out whooshed liquid, all over me, the settee cushion and the carpet. And this is me dressed. I made it to the bathroom and my jug before the next outpouring. Two litres may have been an underestimate considering how much was lost to measuring in the lounge outburst. Pre-bed I upped the loperamide from two to three four times a day. Was I really supposed to twiddle with the loperamide dosage so often? Guidance? Get away with you ... heal yourself sucker.

Not to worry, I had a consultation with Mary-Jane in a week's time. And although my stoma bags were watertight over the next couple of days the discharge was water so I upped the loperamide again, back to four, four times a day, back to what Mary-Jane's team had put me on at the beginning of November. Well, in charge I was.

*

Was there an element of stroppy for stroppy's sake? Definitely not at the time, though I can see, looking back, why that might be thought to be the case. At the time I felt both defeated and neglected. And *clinical nurse specialist, stoma care* was a very hard to swallow joke. Talk about nine to five, Monday to Friday. Leave a message after the beep … better still phone someone who cares. Actually, try and phone someone who not only cares but can help, for caring in itself is not enough. Good luck.

Too harsh? Great expectations? Expectations that the stoma nurses initially gave me, that I left hospital with … but my New Year experience ended any remaining sense that they actually had the power, wherewithal or knowledge to care.

This was my first thing (overnight, or pre-dawn) email to the stoma nurses of the 4th of January.

Happy New Year!

Please find below a copy of my letter to Ms Mary-Jane, posted today, in readiness for my appointment next week.

FYI – I have been in agony – it was 4AM last night before my intestines stopped behaving like a washing machine with no off switch. The laxative/loperamide game of twist or stick is a game I cannot play!

Neil.

4th January, 2022.
Ms Mary-Jane,
Colorectal Surgery,
Princess Royal University Hospital,
Farnborough Common,
Orpington,
Kent,
BR6 8ND.

Dear Ms Mary-Jane or Colorectal Surgery team member,

Hospital Number Mxxxxxx - NHS Number xxxxxxxxxx – Neil Andrews

I thought it would be useful for you to have my current list of questions prior to my appointment on the 14th.

I would see 3 main objectives for Jan 14:

1. Confirmation that operation to remove the blockage has achieved the desired outcome & there are no additional complications caused by the operation?
2. Confirmation that there is no reason at this present time why the stoma reversal will not go ahead as expected in April?
3. What course of action would you advise when the intermittent stomach cramps occur, simply waiting for the excruciating pain to pass is insufferable & impacts other aspects of my general health?

Latest update since drafting the above: I spent the night of 1st, morning of 2nd January in A&E, ending up for the last five hours in SA&A Unit where I was advised that I was constipated and recommended suppositories and/or laxatives. I was surprised at the duty doctor's suppository suggestion. As it happens the nurse said they had none, and I said I had a supply of *Laxido* at home. Since my return home I have administered myself with *Laxido*. [I do not have the vocabulary to express what I went through last night into this morning, both physically and emotionally.] I feel that everything is a constant trial & reset rather than following a recommended approach & sticking with it?

Yours,

Hi Neil

I will forward your letter to Miss Mary-Janes email.
I have read the notes regarding your visit to A+E- not a good start your year I'm sorry you had to come in.
I would advise you to stop the Laxido, its action is to draw more water into the bowel to soften stool which you do not need and won't help with your symptoms.
Please give me a call if you want to run through symptoms and we can advise.

Kind regards,
Stoma Nurse A.

My telephone call on the 4th triggered this email chain …

Hi Stoma Nurse A, I appreciated chatting yesterday and I feel the after effects of the Laxido have nearly all gone, last night was much more peaceful.

On the point of leaving the SA&A unit on Sunday I noticed my bag had leaked. The nurse, Brylle, was surprised that I was not supplied with some stronger tape, *banana band* I think he called it. I see it mentioned online but I am unsure what it comes under from the Fittleworth products listed on their website. The leaks are predominantly opposite my navel where my body shape has a hollow kink now. Can you advise? Thanks.

Will you be attending my appointment on the 14th?

Banana band, strips, splits, bread … for something's sake! But patience, all shall be revealed …

> *Dear Neil,*
>
> *I am pleased you are feeling a little better.*
>
> *The ' bananas' you mention are flange extenders, designed to give a bit more security around the edge of the pouch.*
>
> *I think we may have tried them at some point perhaps while you were still an inpatient, but didn't need to continue with them at that time.*
>
> *They can help with securing the pouch - particularly if you have dips in the abdomen.*
>
> *You can order some samples directly from the companies, or I can send you some to try, and if you find them useful, they can be added to your regular order from Fittleworth.*

We would not routinely be at your appointment with Miss Mary-Jane.

Best wishes,

Stoma Nurse B.

Fair enough …

Hello Stoma Nurse B,

Thanks for this info. A few examples would be useful as the 'dips' seem to be increasing as the stoma shrinks and as I lose more weight.

Kind regards,
Neil.

Stoma love letters? Behave Nels!

Dear Neil,

I shall pop some in the post for you to try.

If they prove useful, let us know and we can add them to you regular order.

Best wishes,

Stoma Nurse B.

*

So, what does Julian look like, I hear you ask? You didn't. Tough!

It is gender neutral but pretty in pink. I lie. To me the colour is an unattractive red and it would not look out of place swaying in the tidal flow as a species of living coral organism on a tropical reef. Its size varies from peach to plum.

It sits slightly up to the right of my navel, but a good bit below the right ribcage … and it oozes excrement like a seabed creature. Though I imagine a seabed creature has sphincter control.

That's Julian for you.

*

It would appear to be an appropriate moment to divulge four days of entries made to the *Stoma Diaries*.

> 7/1
> 2 Imodium at 07:45, cornflakes.

2 Imodium at 12:15, cheese in toasted bagel.

2 Imodium at 18:10, salmon and penne.

What is the point of the diet – over TWO litres of liquid discharge with penne confetti.

3 Imodium at 22:30, biscuits.

<u>8/1</u>
62.75kgs.

3 Imodium at 08:31, cornflakes with stewed apples.

Stinky porridge consistency discharge, at least last night's 2+ litres wasn't too smelly. Relativity. ☺

Have the marshmallows kicked in? How long will this bag remain shit-tight?

3 Imodium at 12:38, cheese in toasted bagel, mashed banana.

3 Imodium at 17:58, salmon and penne, strawberry yoghurt.

Dreading going to bed as no stoma action all day …

3 Imodium at 21:10.

9/1
3 Imodium at 08:17, cornflakes with stewed apples.

Porridge consistency, dry night. Phew! First 24+ hours bag for weeks.

Continued porridge consistency discharge.

3 Imodium at 12:11, cheese in toasted white bread, strawberry yoghurt.

3 Imodium at 17:03, Val's roast pork dinner.

3 Imodium at 21:03, over a litre of liquid discharge this evening regardless of the marshmallows!

<u>10/1</u>
3 Imodium at 07:37, cornflakes with stewed apples.

Let's hope we can get on the two-day bag change cycle again!

64.6kgs

4 Imodium at 12:26, cheese in toasted white bread rolls.

4 Imodium at 18:09, spaghetti carbonara, rhubarb yoghurt.

4 Imodium at 22:02, 3 plus litres of liquid despite a bag of jelly babies and hula hoops. Feeling very dehydrated.

It captured such a variety of emotions as well as recording the doubling of my loperamide intake over the days involved, yet with seemingly no effect on my stoma discharge. The joy of a dry night, and a stoma bag remaining in situ for more than twenty-four hours; followed by the disbelief at the metric volume of my liquid discharge regardless of the prescribed thickening ingredients.

Thus was my life measured.

All my fault, obviously. Fucking AMC! And so, the stoma nurses can walk away as they have done all they can. Neil, just deal with it.

And I did deal with it, even though the depression of December had not exactly shifted, how could it after my New Year celebrations, but I was now over halfway through the six months before reversal. Take whatever positives were on offer. Even if fabrications of my own creation derived from the wishful thinking of my propensity for a blue-sky temperament.

*

10/1 email, and I am not a happy bunny …

Good morning!

Well, the good news is that from yesterday morning I started to feel somewhat better for the first time in 2022 and probably since 27th December.

However, as I recover the more annoyed, I feel at my prescriptive advice from the doctor in the SA&AU on 2nd. The physical and emotional trauma I went through on the evening, night/morning of 3rd/4th needs reporting. The 'end game' to this trauma was potentially Friday night as my bag discharged over 2 litres of liquid within half an hour ... not, may I add, contained by bag or clothing (use your imagination ...).

What is potentially interesting is that on the Friday and Saturday I ate identical food, happy to forward my 'stoma diaries' to you – and after Friday's dam burst Saturday was porridge thick discharge. (Last night a reversion back to over 1 litre of liquid, thankfully not in one wave.)

Apologies Stoma Nurse B if, whilst in hospital, I rejected 'banana'

Stoma in a teacup

strips, I cannot recall, not that I actually feel I need to apologise, as I was probably so fixated with what my fingers had to contend to with the bags themselves. Interestingly, or pointedly for me with my disability, the bag Stoma Nurse A last attached and that nurse Brylle attached on 2nd both leaked across from my navel. I rest my case, body shape not application.

Talking of body shape my weight is now 62.60kgs. Whether having an appetite again will see this rise I question, as I have forced myself to eat regardless. Over to you?

Is it over to you though? I have no longer, if I ever did, any idea of who THE DUTY OF CARE of me falls under, my GP thinks yourselves!

As you will be aware Friday's consultation is now to be by telephone, presumably Ms Mary-Jane (or colleague) will ask me to press around my own stomach and go 'ouch' as appropriate. Sarcasm aside I am relieved that it is 'only' the appointment format that has been changed as opposed to an outright cancellation as my pre-appointment questions stand. If you have kept with this email so far, and my rant is not personal, but at the sheer FRUSTRATION of coping on MY OWN, do you think a photo of the stoma would be useful for Ms Mary-Jane (or colleague) to view whilst talking to me?

This morning, the area around the stoma seems more rounded than with the troughs of recent times – let's hope this morning's bag application allows me to return to my forty-eight-hour bag change routine and a sense of my pre-Christmas normality.

Have a good week.

Kind regards,
Neil.

How to rattle invisible cage bars …
Good Morning, Andrew, [Oh dear! See?]

Glad to hear you are feeling a bit better.

You are probably right that we were trying to keep the pouch and accessories as simple as possible in those early days.

I have posted some of the flange extenders to you, see how you get on with them.

In terms of 'Duty of care', that is something that applies to all professionals involved in your care, including your GP. Once out of hospital and at home, the regular care falls to your GP, but in more complex cases (such as yourself) this is always a collaborative approach.

A photo of your abdomen will always be useful for Miss Mary-Jane's consultation, and might help with your 'self-examination'!!

Best Wishes,

Stoma Nurse B.

I duly submitted a photograph of Julian, pretty in cherry-red as opposed to pink.

*

For once an email to someone other than either Stoma Nurse A or Stoma Nurse B, to Karen.

> Good morning – amazing – first double forty-eight-hour turnaround of morning-shower-bag-change routine for AGES!
>
> Was in process of speaking to Mary-Jane's secretary when your message came through – have now emailed two photos of Julian to her.
>
> The discharge is a complete mystery. All I need now is to be able to relax in bed rather than wake up feeling around for leaks. Little by little rebuild in confidence, I guess. Tony's coming round this morning to see if he can fix doorbell, but think my Julian selfies are okay.

Silence from the stoma nurses, so much ref DUTY OF CARE with regards to weight loss.

WOW! Kevin is on a charge – it is an easy but page turning read. Christine bought it for me. [Referring to *Hallowed Ground* by Paul Twivy.] Too busy on draft six [*Absolution in Neutral*] here to get back to my Dracula read. [*The Historian* by Elizabeth Kostova.]

Love,

Neil.

*

And here we were, for Tony had come over from Essex, and we recorded the near twenty-minutes of the Mary-Jane phone consultation of January 14th. I had prepped the questions I wanted answers to and Mary-Jane had Stoma Nurse A beside her. I had forwarded my questions in advance as well as an up-to-date photo of the sitting pretty stoma.

Two-thirds of the way through the consultation I decided it was time to interrupt Mary-Jane's flow, which generally had nothing to do with my questions, and advise her that my name was Neil not Andrew! It was bad enough the Stoma Nurse B calling me Andrew but to have the consultant say it over and over again. In all my dealing with her she never quite kicked the habit.

Obviously COVID-19 still had a lot to answer for, as well as cover up.

Whilst January progressed my bag leaks did not cease, thus the email exchange that commenced on January 18th ...

> *Sorry to hear you have had such terrible night.*
>
> *Yes, give us a call on Wednesday. I think we should try you on some different bags to try and see if we can get on top of the leaks.*
>
> *We can leave some for you to collect at the main reception of the hospital, but call on Wednesday so we can discuss.*
>
> *Kind regards*

Stoma Nurse A.

With my response as follows ….
Hi Stoma Nurses A and B – is tomorrow's appointment primarily to see if I need a reduced circumference for my stoma bags? (Just wondering if I need to bring anything with me.) Thanks, Neil.

[Oh! the urge to add … apart from my wit and flippancy!]

Dear Neil,

as I understand it, yes, it is to resize your template.

It's always good to bring a small kit with you anyway, and we can compare your current template.

See you tomorrow.

Stoma Nurse B.

*

Hopefully the flange extenders will arrive today,

so I can start to experiment … I do not think I should need to wake thankful that I have made it through another unsoiled night over three months after the op.

Flange Extenders – and this mind of mine thinks of interesting book titles, with minimal substance, obviously, as it's Mr Flippant here, and all the substance, dietary goodness, flows out of me …

*

Another email bleats its way to Karen's inbox.

Bag decides to open from below last night at 7ish, whilst I am beavering away at the novel … didn't realise at first. Managed to do shower-to-fresh-bag in a discharge gap ☺ – but perhaps did not apply or dry properly as up at 3 with a leak – back to usual navel spot – despite me actually applying a banana strip. And eating a mass of marshmallows after the evening leak. Sticking to 4x4 as discharge less porridge like again.

But, thankfully, in a better place

Stoma in a teacup

mentally …hopefully.

Hope you had a good day in Streatham.

Bag leaked in a new place in the night – LOL! (LOL! Totally inappropriate- bloody modern speak!!!!) Definitely sticking to 4x4 as jolly liquid again. Despite marshmallows!

Weight up, which is positive, stoma nurses phoned this afternoon so seeing them at 3PM on Wednesday at the hospital – interesting when I couldn't be seen by the consultant. Behave Neil.

Had a bridge four here this afternoon and apart from winning was also good for the spirits.

And another glorious day, had hygienist this morning, walked both ways without my stick.

Yes Person-in-Charge, how come the stoma nurses can see me facemask-to-facemask but Mary-Jane can't?

*

Loving this example of my gratitude for small

mercies … I really needed to get out more …
<u>17/1</u>
65.6kgs upwards

4 Imodium at 07:36, peanut butter
on white toast.

4 Imodium at 12:10, soft goats'
cheese in two white rolls, rhubarb
yoghurt.

4 Imodium at 18:30, fish pie.

Over two litres of liquid –
thankfully captured at the wash
handbasin.

4 Imodium at 22:25.

*

Part of me so, so wanted to chicken out. So, wanted! It was a cold Thursday night in January. What was I thinking of? Yes, this was our fourth attempt to see *Pretty Woman*, the musical. Originally booked for 2020 and here we now were in January 2022.

Stoma in a teacup

Yet, I know. Crazy! The Gemini in me? Yet, part of me wanted to go. To show? To prove? What had I to prove? And to whom? There was just me. Everyone else knew I was nuts.

But all my friends are special, and that is how I aim to make them feel, and Debbie so wanted to see this show. Her favourite film translated into a musical. How would my stoma behave? Would it behave? As if not on edge enough the train came to a standstill at Waterloo East station. Yes, it was a stopping point, but neither (quite) the tipping point nor its (nor my) destination, that was Charing Cross. There was a trespasser on the line. What the ****? During the rush hour too. We were advised to disembark as the train was unlikely to be moving forward anytime soon.

I duly did decant myself, and made my way gingerly along to Waterloo Bridge, yet too speedily for someone who wasn't yet used to using a crutch. I seemed to feel the cold rising off The Thames go through the layers of clothing. A cap was not a warm enough covering for my head.

On purpose, I had had nothing to eat since an

early lunch consisting of Pam's homemade soup accompanied by dry white bread toast. I had a cheese sandwich in my man-bag for the journey home. There was no way I wanted a theatre discharge. I wanted Debbie to be able to enjoy the show, not have her in turn worry about my angst.

It was quite a rowdy audience. Literally bottles of wine where being taken to seats, and after the interval there was minor scuffling in the last two rows of the stalls. At least Debbie knew me well enough to have a drink herself despite my own *thank you but no*. I had to get through this.

And I did. The stoma bag behaved and I ate my sandwich at ten-thirty on the train home. Sue H and I used to joke about avoiding the Tunbridge Wells trains because of all the food smells. And here was I joining the munchers.

So do I give myself a tick, a pat on the back or but a shake of the head at my sheer bloody mindedness. Probably a mixture.

Nine days later and I was back at it. Theatre going that is. *La Belle Sauvage* at The Bridge, but a mere one-month COVID delay from this

Stoma in a teacup

outing's original booking.

Practice makes perfect! Well, no, but it does enable a level of relaxation. And as Louise noted I was able to relax during the second half of a brilliantly conceived production of a novel set upon the flooded Thames. A belated Christmas with The Hales, what am I going to do when the last of their children is too old for thinking of a Christmas theatre outing as a treat?

Amongst the initial pack that the stoma nurses gave on their visit to my bedside in the PRUH was a key. The R.A.D.A.R. key scheme for access to disabled toilets, the ones that are locked, like in railway stations or pubs or some theatres; some toilets for the disabled in theatres don't use this key scheme. The Bridge doesn't, which is fine as long as the toilet isn't abused by queue jumpers … as I have seen happen at the Royal Opera House. Funny that no-one had ever before suggested that I should be in possession of such a key. What I have discovered though is that if you are locked inside, using one of these toilets anyone with a key can let themselves in to join you. Online it suggests knocking before entry. Excuse me, if that's the expected practice why are there not big signs, such as KNOCK

BEFORE UNLOCKING, plastered on the door.

Thankfully the one-time (so far) when I was intruded upon by a non-knocker-first, at the Hammersmith Apollo, I was in the later stages of my toileting, so there was no exposure. Though I got glared at for not locking the door … I politely but curtly explained. In this day and age of health and safety obsessiveness is there not an issue here about unsavoury key holders intruding upon minors …

R.A.D.A.R. keys are available on Ebay!!!!!!!

As for the modern woke semantics, *accessible toilets* … aren't all the toilets accessible. Please, please, please. We are well passed 1984 and newspeak.

February 2022

Let's start the new month off with an email as opposed to a bang; for the bang had already occurred.

Good morning!

Yes, it is really approaching 4AM and I am on my third bag of the night – the middle one lasted 90 minutes – pristine clean internally apart from its chosen *9 o'clock to navel* escape route … the same route they all seem to choose.

Are all bags similar from this regard, with just the discharge opening different, for as discussed previously it doesn't appear to be an application issue? If it is an application error then I certainly need this stoma reversed on the 6th of April.

Perhaps we can talk on Wednesday? I have a funeral to attend later this morning – not my own just yet. ☹

Neil.

Was I just, to quote a former work colleague, pissing in the wind?

The 1st of February response
Hi Neil

Sorry to hear you have had such terrible night.

Yes, give us a call on Wednesday. I think we should try you on some different bags to try and see if we can get on top of the leaks.

*We can leave some for you to
collect at the main reception of the
hospital, but call on Wednesday
so we can discuss.*

Kind regards

Stoma Nurse A

Trying to play nice is quite trying!
Will do. Thanks Stoma Nurse A –
though it might be worth looking at
the stoma shape as well as that
part of my body. Can the stoma
grow as well as shrink, as it
seems a tighter fit since last
week?

Neil.

Let us add peristalsis to the mix …
Hi Neil

*Certainly, the stoma can grow as
well as shrink, as the bowel
naturally contracts and relaxes as
a part of peristalsis (movement of
the bowel.)*

We can speak on Wednesday and talk through some options to try.

Kind regards

Stoma Nurse A

*

Time me thinks for further extracts from the *Stoma Diaries* …

<u>5/2</u>

Overnight bag leak – usual navel discharge escape.

4 Imodium at 07:08, white bread with shredless spread.

4 Imodium at 11:59, cheese sandwich on white bread, fluffy pudding.

4 Imodium at 17:56, chicken, bacon, leek pie, fluffy pudding.

4 Imodium at 22:10.

I DID KEEP A RECORD FOR THESE FIVE

DAYS, BUT MANAGED TO LOSE IT (AS IN NOT SAVE IT) ... THOUGH FOR SOME REASON I KNOW MY WEIGHT WAS 65.75KGS ON THE 7TH.

11/2
After a night of endless bag changes so tired.

4 Imodium at 07:10, white bread with shredless spread.

4 Imodium at 13:09, prawn sandwich, two ciabatta rolls.

4 Imodium at 17:13, trout fillet and puffed hula hoops!

4 Imodium at 22:58.

Dreading bed!

Blimey, obviously the start of February saw a storm of a stoma from my perspective, yet I cannot recall why, other than the vagaries of my PC (and it does have its moments), I would lose five days of my meticulously kept *Stoma Diaries*, especially when it appears such a hiatus of a time. I have included this particular excerpt for I believe it shows via the last two words the draining effect. Going to bed should ideally be a recuperative process in readiness for the next day, however if you are dreading going to bed you are not going to exactly have a calm and restful night. That constant dread of seeping dampness, or woken by my nose knowing what has been permeating under the bedclothes.

Whilst the *Stoma Diaries* showed that I followed the above hiatus with a good spell of dry nights it also revealed that I was waking-up, as well as actually getting up, earlier and earlier. Therefore, curtailing my sleeping time so as to avoid leakages. Now that's neither right nor healthy. And hardly sustainable.

How true …

With the winter Olympics occurring it's satisfying to achieve a PB – six bag changes in just over twenty-four hours … I know, must try harder.

The delight though in waking up as Neil and the chocolate poo factory.

Today's out of the house tasks; fill up the petrol

Stoma in a teacup

tank and buy compost for Bill and/or Ben to decant from the car tomorrow. It was whilst filling up with petrol that I felt that the ongoing discharge was not being contained within bag five of the six.

Bag leakage that has suddenly changed tack, as though hearing my claims as the previous ones were defeating the laws of gravity. All current leaks head due south. I wondered if I was over enthusiastic with my opening of the discharge escape chute. No, can't be, as some bags have leaked before any Neil discharge release.

Anyway, was I to be defeated. No. Back home I drove, seat protected by a plastic car boot sheet and after a change of clothes and general clean-up off I set. Clothes washing had to wait, the washing machine was still busy …

Three fifty litre bags of peat free compost now nestled in my boot and I was back home. The sixth bag holding solid, so to speak.

Should I recant? Hell no!

Safe in the arms of Jesus – still one of God's children. Amen.

Neil Raffan

*

What was it with my gardeners, actually now my ex-gardeners, and bad news Mondays? Was this why or how I lost days of entries into the *Stoma Diaries*?

Actually!

Yes, true, after their visit of Monday 4th October was when I took ill. But Bill's announcement on Monday 7th February was a veritable kick in the stoma. The facts. Okay, I accept my take on reality. Since their visit of 4th October, I had virtually left them to their own devices, either from being in hospital or not being well enough to garden. I reckon the first Monday in February may have been about the second time since October that I gardened alongside them. Them is a euphemism here as it was actually Ben I assisted as Bill was obviously in a huff. Bill was flaky in this way. Yes, we all have our ups and downs, good days and bad days, but when you are in the people business etc.

Interesting, as I had been told of Bill and Ben's existence via a fellow member of the tennis club;

who the men stopped working for as they didn't like his attitude ... ungrateful grumpiness. Allegedly! After giggling at this piece of unnecessary news I did ask that they advise me if there were any such issues ... but it seemed that I was *a breath of fresh air* as my annual newsletters testify by dint of complimenting them on their work.

So, back to this particular fateful Monday. Usually, Bill did creative gardening whilst Ben was given the muscle jobs; as a rule, that is, for Bill was the gardener and by profession Ben was an NHS carer nurse. However, Bill took it upon his non-communicating self to do the left-over shredding of the James Roof garrya, whilst Ben and I arranged the planting of the bed they had been clearing over the autumn (under instruction but in my absence). The fact I noted Bill's mood must have meant at some level it affected me. I asked Ben to check with Bill that he was happy with our planned plant positioning, the response being that my placing would be as good as his. At this point I enquired of Ben as to what was up? To which he disingenuously replied that they had had a heated argument in the van en route to me. Boys will be boys, so I thought.

I was still physically incapable of doing a full two hours of gardening so had retired indoors and made a payment by bank transfer by the time Bill asked to have a word at my back door prior to their departure. I was not to see Ben again. I state this here as to my mind he has the key to the mystery that follows. Bill announced that they would no longer be gardening for me as I showed no sign of appreciating his work and he could no longer work under such stressful conditions, to the extent that Ben and he had had a major barney on the way up from Tunbridge Wells. Knock me down with a feather. Well, I am gay! I disputed this view of my appreciation, knowing full well that I thanked and praised him on his work. Genuinely too, for I loved his sculpting of my pittosporum, choisya and euonymus shrubbery bed. I had also given him glowing referrals.

Obviously, my own mental condition as a result of my physical one did not help but I was knocked for six by this, and though I asked him to think it through for the fortnight before their next scheduled visit deep within I knew that was that. Which it was.

Nevertheless, I churned his accusations over

and over, looking for moments when I had been ungrateful. If he had mentioned my joke over the most expensive wisteria or something that I disagreed with him over underlying horticultural knowledge, fair enough … but nothing but the atmosphere that he could no longer work in.

My own take? With whatever issues Bill had going on upstairs, as per mood swings, unless he did actually believe that contrary to all evidence, I did not think he was doing a grand job, my belief is that he had somehow contrived to perceive that I was *after* Ben. Interesting! Inuendo was common parlance amongst the three of us; but not only was Bill the most obvious but also generally the instigator. Yes, hands up, I preferred Ben … but not in *that* way, to chat to about gardening.

In time, and most definitely once their replacement had started, I realised how gardening with Bill had been an emotional strain for me. Retrospectively amusing.

Having but Bill's contact details there was no way of accessing the key that Ben may have to help with the actual truth of it all. Even unlocked would Ben's truth match mine? Or was there a further variation on the theme waiting to be aired?

One of my many weaknesses is feeling guilty even when innocent and Bill's accusations had this effect on me for quite some time afterwards. The bastard!

I kept replaying their years of work here. Yes, years. And no *by the way Neil, if you don't appreciate our efforts, we'll be off* warning. Looking back, I see two things, how flaky Bill always was and how accommodating I was. Any drop of rain and they would cancel as working conditions would be too dangerous; sick days; time keeping was not something they had any management over. The other side of this, my acceptance, tolerance (the forever broken scarifier), genuine sympathy over their dog's ill-health and ultimate demise. With regard to the latter much more than Ben's heavy-handedness five months, yes five months, after Sun's death. Yet six weeks before resigning Bill had thanked me for the year's work whilst receiving his Christmas box.

Man did it gnaw at me. I knew this would wear off given time but knowing how little I could do physically the need to find replacements seemed like another burden. One I genuinely felt I did not deserve to be carrying. Yet, as I was all too inclined to do, I trawled through conversations and visits that could possibly have led to Bill's own trauma.

As all those people I keep in touch with can testify, I hate letting go. I can only think of two people in my whole adult life where I have been the one who actively chose to do so. With others whose choice was to drop me I have been known to even write return addresses on Christmas card envelopes, just in case …

But there was no way I was going to inveigle my way inside Bill's head. Let it go. Accept it is inside his head. Full stop.

That good old friend, time. And then to smile and laugh about when others tell you of their own perception of Bill's personality irrespective of garden prowess … cold, on his guard, unsmiling …

And I did move on. Physically much quicker than emotionally, in that I employed a replacement gardener before inaccurately self-inflicted

Schadenfreude had worn out … sort of.

The trouble was, *sort of* knowing that a conversation with Ben would potentially answer my question still lingered. Sort of, for it very well may not. Not if he believed Bill's take on their time working for me. And my bottom line with Ben was his cowardliness in not being party to the farewell. And there I drew my own line under it.

Joe became my new gardener. A single man, probably ten to fifteen years younger than either of his predecessors. More expensive per hour but a much faster worker. Very open in attitude and calm temperament, in all weathers.

I must remain on my guard though, for months Joe had also stated what a good boss I am …

What does that actually mean, I wonder? He made this statement to me after over six months in my employ post an exchange with the plumber who was converting my bathroom into a wet-room. My take, yes, learn to realise it is your own take, honest, decent and above all treat as you would appreciate being treated.

Stoma in a teacup

*

I must admit that it was a shock. I had assumed that the stoma nurses had disclosed everything I needed to know about dealing with my stoma. Their reticence was being blamed on my AMC. I could partly grok this as their initial empathy was based on the dexterity issues that I faced with attaching the stoma bags. To a large extent that part of the process was relatively easy. RELATIVELY in capitals. And glibly, it is all relative. But hadn't they complimented me on my stoma bag attaching; even though their praise was initially misplaced encouragement, as those *yes, you've got it* initial bag placements leaked well before their ideal, that is my standard measurement, forty-eight-hour cycle. The point is, I am getting there, is that they had never seen me have to deal with a faeces fountain. The issue may still be placed on the doorstep of AMC but not at the dexterity level ... look at how I cleaned up my shit. Look, but hold your nose. Flippant! Focus? Okay! Wasn't the issue an ileostomy combined with my physiognomy – the perfect storm?

During my initial October 2021 fortnight in hospital there was a third stoma nurse, but

Stoma Nurse C was neither seen nor heard thereafter. I do however remember a look she gave when, pre-discharge, the question was asked how I was managing with the stoma bag application. Trepidation for what lay ahead, was what I read from her concerned look, but it was already what I felt and hospital escape was paramount. With the beauty of hindsight, I do not think extended hospitalisation would have actually assisted with the day-to-day living with a post-ileostomy stoma ... as the worsening of the leaks commenced well after the operation.

So, I therefore did what I recommend people not to do. I went over to the dark side. Internet searching. No excuse, no justification, but there is mitigation ... my search was limited to stoma bags and their accoutrements. I discovered a whole industry.

Doreen had had a stoma since her bowel cancer op. Hers was to the left and below her navel, so lower intestine, whereas mine was above and to the right of my navel. The stoma bags she had been kitted out with had no emptying outlet. And Doreen generally reported that the content was usually normal solid poo that one would expect one's bottom to produce. This I NEVER

202

achieved. Doreen's only exceptions being when she had bouts of diarrhoea. Doreen could not help herself, she was addicted to nuts, therefore was prone to the squirts when she over indulged.

There was almost a shopping-on-Amazon like sensation with the stoma accessory world, as long as it was listed in Fittleworth's extensive catalogue it was accessible. And even if it wasn't there were other suppliers out there offering free samples of their wares.

Go stoma go! Innovate! Accessorise!

And I did, well, as I was having trouble with the proffered fixtures and fittings why not see if there was anything more suitable to my needs out there. So, Dear Reader, yes YOU, I know you can't wait! So, here goes, stoma bags I have known …

Three encased bags: -

There is the *pelican platinum with vitamin E* no less. This stoma bag has a plugged discharge facility. Quite handy if your discharge is liquid or has a slight viscosity but awful if you reach the desired porridge consistency, which makes one wonder about the design in the first place. *Dedicated to stoma care – MADE IN BRITAIN* but with no consideration given to patient needs, obviously.

The *Dansac 3081-54* is quite similar to my regular *Dansac Nova REF 816-15*, other than the raised stoma encasement, being opaque and the Velcro opening once sealed being less accessible. The area of adhesion appears greater than with the *Nova*, but appearances can be deceptive. I knew someone who used to drive a Vauxhall Nova … Neil, this is boring enough without irrelevant interjections. Focus, please.

The *Confidence BE* appears to me as a feminine bag (without wishing to appear as being non-PC), it is the smallest of these three, therefore less obtrusive, provided by Salts healthcare, with a Velcro secured discharge opening. To adhere the bag the adhesive sections are quartered, which does ease adhesion but likewise eases exit access for leaks.

These three all had opaque covers, so one could not view the discharge beforehand. Personally, and this was not some weird fetish that I had added to my psyche, I just liked some inkling of what was about to exit as I discharged into a plastic jug with a litre capacity. This bag also came with eyes that a belt with hooks could support. In my own experience the belt became unhooked. My fault, obviously, AMC or post-op body shape, but I could imagine how the belt would be a comfort should one's bag fill to capacity and one feared it coming unstuck through the natural law of gravity. Gravity!

As stated, my regular bag had been the *Dansac Nova REF 816-15*. My **only** issue with it has been the leaks. I liked the visibility of content and I found the emptying the easiest (relative, obviously). With my level of wind/gas - capacity of all bags was an issue. My main issue with this bag was the propensity to leak, even when not prostrate the bag seemed to leak on a line across to my navel. I could only assume body shape and stoma exit hole had something to do with this.

Before giving them the thumbs down I tried two of the *Pelican Platinum* model. I actually got on quite well with the *tap* from the manual dexterity aspect. However, the issue with the tap was that if your discharge was of a thick porridge consistency, you cannot but help create air gaps as you try and empty the bag, which become liquid gaps. Both bags leaked within 24 hours. The second time in the traditional navel spot – which I contained for a further 24 hours with the banana strips, but that so wasn't the point …

Though I managed the belt it would hook off of its own accord during the day.

Though the plastic covering was harder to remove of the *Salts Healthcare – Confidence BE* I liked the cuts in the outer ringer for ease of sticking down. The opening may prove tricky and the bag may prove to be too small for you, if your output is as extensive as mine. Sadly, a leak occurred within but a couple of hours – the downside of the ease of application. Have tried the longer banana sticky as a seal! But again, not the point.

Stoma in a teacup

And on the Neil trials went …

A fourth encased bag was sent to me as a free sample, actually three of them by a very pleasant Sam at Amcare.

> The *Convatec VO 422159* bag itself fitted well, which is excellent considering the measurements were relayed over the phone. The bag capacity however is less than my DANSAC bag of choice and the discharge exit has additional folds.

But, during its trial the discharge chute lost its Velcro adhesion and thus the contents emptied down my right trouser leg. I was dead-heading and pruning my hydrangeas. No, I refuse to make any comments other than the summer's drought that was to follow did the hydrangeas more damage. Since, when I ensured the seal was properly stuck closed the issue became a dexterity challenge to release it.

Thus ended the trials and though pleased that I had tried, it was a case of the devil you knew, in my case the *Dansac Nova REF 816-15.*

For the lay person it is probably easiest to compare my manual dexterity to that of someone with chronic rheumatoid arthritis. I don't do fiddly things! I find picking up stray pills that dance their way across the kitchen worktop a challenge. I handle the cutlery I use daily better than that of friends or eateries. And though an arthritis sufferer has lost their previous dexterity, over time mine too has diminished. To think that thirty plus years ago I learnt to use chopsticks in my Tokyo hotel by picking up Treets (before they became M&Ms)! I can no longer use chopsticks, thankfully this is not life threatening. Nor is losing the ability to wipe one's own bottom, but it is a fear.

*

The bright side! Yes, I do know how annoying it and, as a result, I can be by always quoting it. *Looking on the bright side …* Today's stroll down to visit my friend Ed a case in point. No distance from my house my left knee, as it is wont to do, gave way on me … and I am floored, or pavemented in this case. Two, or potentially three, actually now I want to list them FOUR bright side thoughts occur; my mittens and jogging pants meant no bloody scars, my collapse had not been witnessed, I could resume an upright stance unaided and I had not fallen into any dog shit. I am truly blessed.

Add to this the fact that my stoma bag merely inflated like a balloon and there's another blessing in itself, for if there had been a passer-by, they would have been spared the fart, both sound and smell, the wind's attempted escape captured by the stoma bag!

And my walk back home was incident free and achieved before the heaven's opened.

Truly one of God's children.

*

On the 24th of February stoma in a teacup is really put in its place by Putin's invasion of Ukraine. I say Putin's because it is one man's megalomania … so depressing, with nothing it seems to be done. One of the main reasons I did not want us to leave the EU …security for Europe … and it has happened.

*

The stoma or the innards continued to bubble quite violently and noisily it seemed to me. So much wind. I kept expecting the bag to burst, but the discharge was minimal and watery. The stoma itself was painful against the sores on the skin, that was because of the bag aperture size I used in the hope of halting the rapid change of bags and this one had been on for over forty-eight hours now – so the plan was to shower and change it tomorrow if the bag held out till then and revert to the tighter fit. Such the conundrums of life with a stoma bag.

*

I am concerned about my friend Ed and the fact that he's virtually stopped eating anything but porridge. He looks worse than he did last week, not better. What to do? Do I drive over to his son's home to express my concern? I don't have his telephone number.

*

Tiredness. I have never known it to be so debilitating. I can hardly move, slow motion such an effort. Fighting, always fighting sleep.

Yawn.

But I mustn't sleep, the bag might burst. Even if I wrap the bag in a hand towel and lie on the quilted plastic backed sheet square. Even. Yes, even if I am wrapped in a hand towel there will still be the same *two wash* cycle required, one bio, the other non-bio. The bio to remove all the shit effectively, the non-bio to diffuse the bio wash sufficiently so as not to spark my eczema. Oh joy, joy, joy.

Of course, I'm depressed. I can't sleep. I wake up guilty from snatches of sleep snatched from my bag surveillance. Knowing that I shall fail and will eventually awake soiled, regardless of the times I wake up dry. The plastic quilted sheet makes me sweat, makes me think I am despoiled even before I am. If I awake after 5 AM then I do not bother returning to sleep. A victory, shallow but taken. You have to. Just have to.

Despair. Oh despair!

Sue G understood, the only one who managed to decipher the cloud within the silver lining. Bless her, and she phoned to confirm her interpretation. Double bless her.

Expletive.

But how come no one else could see that there would be no reversal unless the body took on a new shape.

Shaped-up! And for expletive's sake, when has my body ever fulfilled the requested shape. There isn't even an AMC mold to slip or even squeeze into. Oh no! We are all haute couture darling – one offs. In my case well off the peg.

And I haven't even mentioned the hospital appointment.

And the letter asking me to attend a physical facemask-to-facemask meeting was a shock, coming barely a month after the *Andrew* telephone call from Mary-Jane. On February 18th I was scheduled to have a face-to-face meeting with Mary-Jane, where had that come from? Grab it though Neil.

It was with Tony's help that I drew up my appointment statement:
1. The stoma nurses are trying all possible solutions but my stoma's

behaviour has them flummoxed. Still no contact from a dietician.

2. How my mental health is affecting my physical health in that lack of sleep is having an accumulative effect ... through leaking stomas.

3. I need assurance that a reversal will happen, so that I can progress with the conversion of my bathroom to a wet-room. If the reversal is not to happen then I would need to re-think my whole living space.

4. Though going private is not something that I really want to consider however in the circumstances the timing of the reversal is so important to me that I have to consider it if NHS waiting times are going to result in long delays and possible cancellations making it unlikely that the reversal will happen by June.

Except it was not Mary-Jane but a bloke taking one for the team! Tony had made it over from Essex. Thank goodness Euripides had made it to work as it was the day of the storm. This stated, no-one had pre-advised that it wouldn't be Mary-Jane I'd be seeing, though the appointment letter did say that it could be one of the team. Team is good. Isn't it? In itself the *surprise* hospital appointment was but the proffering of a placebo. To be fair to Euripides … fair that is other than changing his name … he managed to suck Tony in to thinking he was about to announce a reversal date whilst in fact all he was doing was being sympathetic to my case. But I was not falling for that, however much Tony might have been taken in by Mary-Jane's Greek Cypriot substitute.

Sympathetic that is until I mentioned the devil's name … GOING PRIVATE! Euripides was very well versed in the NHS hymn sheet when I mentioned going private as a counter to his how long is a piece of string when I questioned the likely length of the NHS wait time for a reversal. Upon which, he stated his commitment to the NHS and no comment. His get-out clause being that I seemed in good enough shape for the reversal not to be delayed on medical grounds. Tony swallowed this. Light, any light. Bravo for you Euripides, but you aren't living with a stoma.

Move on, move on … yes Tony, you were right. We both were. You on the positives that a reversal was mentioned and that I was passed fit. I was right in that there was no semblance of a date.

Tony had dropped me off. Literally, he couldn't stop because of the impending arrival of storm *Eunice*! Expletive, my bottom, my stoma in a teacup ... but pleased to report that he made it back home to Essex before the full force of *Eunice* hit the south-east of England.

I piqued!

And whether the build-up stress or not was with regards to the appointment I had stomach cramps for the rest of the day and the bag's contents was mostly gas with dribbles of clear consommé like discharge. I did nearly phone Tony, but didn't. Make my own decisions.

No loperamide before bed, the cramps had continued and all I wanted to do was curl up and ... sleep. (Fooled you.)

Pay back in the morning, the stoma bag was literally falling off of me, no need today for the spray to release the adhesive. Shit ran down my pyjamas' bottoms, the inside and outside of the wash hand basin, then as I dashed to the loo, all over the loo and the floor surround as the stoma behaved as though an on-the-blink water pistol.

A litre of liquid. Thank goodness I was able to reach the bathroom basin. Can you imagine if that had exploded whilst I was still recumbent in bed? Actually, I dare not imagine? I dare not.

Ever so thankful this morning to realise that I was still one of God's children. I am no longer that supine five-year-old. Jesus loves me, He loves me not …

The upshot of the hospital consultation was an email from Kings (the parent hospital in the Trust that managed the PRUH) via Synopsis, their outsourced provider, asking me to complete the pre-op medical history/statement. Which I duly did by return email. Hopes raised! Hopes dashed! Though Euripides had kick-started this the process then froze. With the life of the pre-admission assessment form about to end I telephoned admissions … there was no known length to the end of the waiting time string … yes, by all means put me on the short notice (forty-eight hours) cancellation list … but in these times who would be foolish enough to cancel an operation? Unless COVID-19 made the decision for them.

What was that reggae song *Long shot kick de bucket*?

*

Naval discharge would appear to be a knuckles typo … naval discharge, and not friendly fire at that. Oh! the fun of scatological humour. *Neil and the chocolate poo factory!* Whilst navel discharge was a reference to the fact that a post ileostomy kink in my body shape seemed to conspire with the majority of my bag leaks occurring across to the right from where my navel blithely sat. An upside with regards to all this mess was that I was less hairy than normal due to pre-operation shave as well as the fact that I had to do my best to keep the area around my stoma as hairless as possible, for hygienic purposes as well as bag adhesion. Such a laugh!

Yet, I do feel anger return, for I consider myself resilient and constantly, for the most part able to fight back but what about those who don't have the emotional fortitude to plough on. I knew Tony feared for my own resolve at times, when I lowered my own guard enough to show a frailty I hated owning. Previously it had only been Karen who had occasionally seen the inside of this tough guy. LOL!

The complete opposite of LOL, for who cares, REALLY CARES. In my very brief experience of Bromley's paid *observers* the actual number of them that could be considered carers was limited to perhaps a couple. I define care as someone who was interested enough and had the ability to ask pertinent questions ... who, if observing was all that their remit consisted of, could actually make sound judgements from said observations. And who you felt could and would escalate issues, your case, if they felt there was a need to. Their visit was not merely a head around your front door with a quick *done* tick to their to-do list. Moving on.

*

I watched a female blackbird under the bird feeder and tried to stay positive. I took a photo with my phone of a beautiful white camellia that has faint pink lines along the tops of its petals and sent it out as *Camellia of the day x* on WhatsApp and tried to stay positive. Trying not to think of Ed or Ukraine. The Ukraine memes have started, didn't take long. Is it wrong to have lost my sense of humour over them? I just wish. Well, that's ridiculous in itself, it isn't JUST what I wish. But I do wish I knew what Putin's bottom line goal is.

I am fourteen again – Prague and Dubček. How I was going to march to the Soviet embassy. How? A disabled fourteen-year-old with feet that walked out of their shoes …

And now very much no longer a child it's the knees for I can no longer walk out of my boots, the Velcro fastening see to that, mostly, except for when the Velcro needs replacing and I have them mended rather than merely replaced. I am not disposable in a world that all too easily adds to its pile of unnecessary trash.

Yes, the knees! Gardening still gives me much contentment; I find it calming as well as giving my being a positive charge. The trouble is, with all this blue-sky positivity there is the need for a reality check. Don't kneel down unless you are using your kneeling frame for otherwise you will not be able to upright yourself. Not a quandary to either find or place yourself in. At the moments when I have nearly forgotten and almost slipped down to my knees unaided in my mind's rush to do a particular spur of the moment task I wonder, how long would it take to raise an alarm, am I dressed for the weather, what is the forecast. This is what it's like to become old, disability aside, for haven't I always been disabled? Where caution is actually sensible, and I am an amazingly self-satisfied individual when it comes down to being sensible, for it is not really me. I have not got where I have today by being cautious …

I know, I know, fabrication. Most of my life has been a cautionary tale of sorts, at least when it comes down to work and the can of worms that is *la vie privée* if not my almost self-harm disregard in the face of initially my parents' and subsequently my friends' friendly advice – DON'T. Anyways, it all seems like an exaggeration, I am on my knees, hardly throwing caution to the wind. I am using my kneeler, that can equally be a seat, with the legs that when used as a kneeler become vital supports for putting me back on my feet. Long may my arms continue to have the strength to do so. Due to my crowded planting style, no bare earth to be seen, kneeling is not always an option, the double over upright planting stance has severe

Stoma in a teacup

limitations in both size of plants that I can physically plant this way, as well as the length of time I can do so. Therefore, much planning is required, or Joe is called upon to do the planting out, tip-toeing amongst the plants that I would clumsily flatten if I attempted the task. These boots are made for squashing! As well as squeaking, but that's another story.

Well okay then, as this is all a story anyway. I put it down to the actual amount of leather in use as opposed to any lack of polishing on my part. The common life denominator – it's not my fault. And my boots do tend to squeak, which was incredibly annoying in the days when I would fork out over £1,700 for a bespoke pair to James Taylor and Son of Paddington Street. How very dare they squeak considering the paid for cost. But they did. Now I just tend to grin when they squeak and the *not paid for* comment is thrown in my direction; for it is technically correct, other than the years of paying tax, as they are provided by the NHS.

*

… and the gardening?

Initially it centred around growing the easy-to-grow annuals ... petunias, pansies, antirrhinums ... the latter were easier to grow than spell. And it transpires that some years snap-dragons behaved as perennials. Then, once I discovered cosmos and sunflowers I was well away. The former providing me with an unsought market place. Such the extent of my nurturing of the cosmos seedings that I had garnered a word-of-mouth demand for these cheerful annuals that, if dead headed, would flower until the first of the autumn frosts.

Though I did grow more ambitious, moving on to the herbaceous perennials I totally failed with delphiniums and lupins, not in the germination stakes but in relation to garden survival. It's a veritable jungle out there and slugs and snails decimated both species. Poppies proved a more successful survivor, the danger for them was overcrowding, they liked space to flourish; a constant reminder to myself as I would tend to fill any patch of bare earth with a fresh planting, the more vigorous of which would fast encroach into poppy-space.

March 2022

COVID catch-up! Such a catch-all. A holdall? What baggage is retained from being healthy, back then, 2019, 2020 … 2021 even, well, I have always had AMC. It's in the condition's description, don't you know? That should be rhetorical, but it isn't, not in this particular case, and to be fair not in previous and subsequent ones either … but as he was a medical practitioner, a hand therapist, should I be fair. Should he not have understood what congenita means? Well, I think he should have and he was lucky that he had such lovely tattoos on his right arm and that I am so shallow as to let him off just because he was *a bit of alright* and I hadn't felt the remotest interest in any of *that* since the ileostomy.

Now tell me, is that subliminal sexual harassment?

I move swiftly on, for I don't give a toss about the answer.

The session with him was another of those NHS outsourcing ones, they did not have enough in-house hand therapists so I was sent to the private sector, located in an adjunct to Fenchurch Street station, nice and local. I took my book for the journey and my plastic litre jug, should there be the need.

The bottom-line reason for seeing him had emanated back in the late summer of 2020 when one of my practice's GPs had asked if I would like to see if there was anything that could be done to arrest the constriction of my fingers into fist balls. I had previously tried a sawed-to-size, by Kevin, wooden rolling-pin. But off and on, dependent on both pain levels and *bothered*. Pre-COVID, the doctor's intervention resulted in the Orpington hospital's surgical appliance gurus providing splints to maintain the fingers extension, for what it is, overnight. But they provided two for the left hand. Obviously. Doesn't everyone have two left hands? Let's be fair here, I have heard it said of people that they have two left feet ...

This chap, with the right arm of colourful tattoos, sent an email of potential aids I could buy to assist stem the inward finger curl. Buy! Well, he is the private sector. I explained to him why, since the ileostomy I had desisted from using the left-hand splints, obviously one at a time, as the disengaging of the three Velcro straps when in a stoma bag leak rush was a palaver for the other hand. Anyway, there was no way I could have used a right hand one at the same time as the left one as I would not have been able to attach it, such the dexterity required.

Back to the right-arm hunk, in the interim I could use any cone shape or even a plastic water bottle to keep the fingers stretched whilst watching television. I could have sworn his actions, demonstrating what he meant, was simulating masturbation but my allotted time was up.

I had a little walk around the area, recalling the

pre-COVID bustle, saddened by the sandwich bar closures; as well as reminiscing of my time as a 2017 World Athletics volunteer, where I was actually based in the guts of The City. The Gherkin has almost been buried within the Cityscape of the now – 2022. A change that cannot be laid at the door of COVID, unlike the emptiness of the trains, the emptiness of The City.

No, I shall not exaggerate, it wasn't like walking around The City on a Sunday. For one thing, on pre-COVID Sundays, tourists in twos and threes would be dotted about the well-thumbed historic streets. But it felt empty, devoid of bustle even if not totally free of workers. It gave the impression that if I shouted out *hello* it would echo around Leadenhall Market and start the inside-out washing machine that is Lloyds churning on a slow spin cycle.

Enough of waxing lyrical. Home with the well-behaved stoma Neil.

*

Good morning! I am literally battling a tide of faeces from filling my surgical boots as my AMC hands struggled with the simultaneity of changing a leaking stoma bag and whilst the stoma continues to discharge.

I jest of course for it is 2AM and I am not feeling it is that good a morning at all … in fact the last twenty-four hours haven't been that great … awake before 5AM yesterday morning (though it still feels like today) to find myself covered in excrement and I am already on my fourth stoma bag (so far) of this particular night.

I actually dread going to bed nowadays, wondering how long it'll be before I wake up either clarted or drenched. With a resulting escalation of tiredness. I've even tried staying up till the stoma has gone to sleep, but it's a sly one and usually manages to con me into a complete false sense of security.

Enough of my badinage … WHAT NEWS ON THE REVERSAL FRONT?

Another 3 litres of dirty dishwater yesterday evening (a lot of standing at my bathroom handbasin), despite a bag of jelly babies. SO, WHO IS LOOKING AFTER MY LOSS OF WEIGHT?

*

Salutary in this will still happen – force of discharge – me unaware etc. … repeated soundbites, gravity will out … I am more aware of wind stretching the bag than of it filling, especially if seated. But there has to be sleep of some sort, there just has to be.

The importance of escape. Even if not real, even if you knew it was not real, but on occasion you had to flee. To leave the confines of your body. And there was a favourite recurring dream, that surprised my waking self. I am on the A96, and on a relatively small or limited stretch of it. The piece from Inverurie to Huntly. That's right, just that small strip of it. The turn-offs and signs float alongside the clouds. But why? Even in a dream state I feel the need to question. The simple answer is the past, but I don't feel that's enough, for I don't see the relevance of this particular chunk of my past in my present. Denial? Can you actually deny a dream's relevance?

Even when wide awake I would have trouble telling you exactly the last time I drove along any part of the A96 let alone this stretch that seems

Stoma in a teacup

to have of late invaded my nights. So much so in fact that I now wonder if I am actually dreaming or am in that pre-sleep stage of visualising the road much travelled in my teen angst years.

But there is blissfully no angst here, the thinness of traffic allows me to gaze, even whilst driving. And I do. I am northbound and the heights are mostly to my left, the lower Cairngorms, with Bennachie eventually moving from the left-hand side to a shrinking vision through the rearview mirror. The VW camper vans have their own dreamland of resurrection at Pitcaple. Now that's not from my youth. Oh no, it's from road trips with Karen and Kevin, and Karen's *thing* about VW camper vans. We were nearly crashed into the first time we came upon the scrapyard, in my adult life, as it's not located at the safest stopping point on the A96, so when she shouted STOP Kevin braked, the car behind was none too pleased but thankfully was able to divert around our *emergency* stop.

Have we passed by the signs to Chapel of Garioch and the Maiden Stone? I know they are on the left, so that's how I see them in this floating drive north, with the turn off to Old Rayne on the right. I am sure in a wide-awake state I would see that some fields do have cattle but in whatever this is, dream or trance, it is sheep, sheep with lambs that may be approaching six months old. Not to be dwelt on.

The sky and the clouds are where I linger, truly mesmerised by the array of shades of grey. There is blue and black, there is slate and silver, there is the whitest white when the sun deigns to shine. The clouds float, they scurry. Patterns of shadow race across the fields to my left, their hue changing from golden to ochre, fresh spring green to a deeper, darker, wet look. I want to capture each blink of the landscape, such the speed of change but the vehicle transporting me seems to have a mind of its own. Onward ever onward, as deciduous and evergreen trees appear and disappear from the roadside, and where have the Insch traffic lights gone? A comparatively flat valley appears to the left here, Insch and beyond, but it's a brief opening, the hills return as further memories return with no summons.

Clatt! Repeating it adds no sense as opposed to likely nonsense which would in effect make sense … but I have no real sense of why Clatt shouts out to me, unlike Drumblade. How could one cycle up to here from Inverurie. What was the road like in those days, I am talking pre-1939, I am talking when women teachers had to resign their posts if they married, I am talking in my sleep ...

Not quite, not at all. I realise that I am not asleep and that I am recalling. Is this what folklore is? Is this gibberish? Should I be dribbling too?

Tales of and from what once had been home. *Bothy Nichts* the dreaded TV show; time for bed, said Zebedee.

The dream sequence digresses from the snowbound A96, turn right for the downhill freewheel to Drumblade. Our days of our own Taliban, women's rights brought upon men by the latter's shortage post 14-18. Calm, sleep, rest – impotent rage as pointless this distant from events as they would have been over one hundred years ago. The distance grows, ever on a relatively small stretch of the A96.

Focus, even in your sleep, on the inexorable beauty of the scene, rolling hills that meet the sky on the horizon, where you wish you were an artist to capture the moment. But no moment can be captured. Gone! Snap … missed it. A vista that you cherish, and realise that however much you poo-poo it, it is in fact imbedded in your psyche. Though in themselves a fact, teenage winters of bronchitis do not detract from the downie that you have wrapped yourself in, smothering the stoma bag within, the moment is Aberdeenshire. An unpretentious landscape that you need to want to see, if you follow, it's neither the Grand Canyon nor Victoria Falls … oops, Mosi-oa-Tunya. It is. And as such it is open to interpretation, perhaps that is both why it is so precious to me right now, as a comforter, but also as a space I recall in various ways – mood dependent. We are made up of recalls, that affect each subsequent recall and so on. At times the tempering condition, others the one that inflames. Man, woman or child … or undecided (woke must out, or in or am I way too confused).

Just, yes just, give me that stretch of the A96 and I shall sleep the sleep of angels, bursting stoma bags be damned.

Obviously, the stoma bags won't be damned, gravity and wind, not to mention their inherent porous selves (which actually, has to be mentioned, and on repeat at that). Good morning, wake up and smell the coffee … oops, smell the bag that has erupted.

And another day starts with you exploring the war zone for peripheral damage. That's the first task, then if it's not catastrophic, as in no extended explosive damage, how to extricate oneself from the envelope that resembles a bed without causing collateral damage to body and soul, body and soil … as in the bedding … or worse if it's a dirty water discharge … soiled body carefully transported by wobbly pins from bedroom to the bathrooms shower … disengaging the smeared midriff from the bedclothes and stoma bag, the latter will be laughing at you through a huge aperture to its side. And I do know, though I have lost the ability to appreciate, that the joke is on me.

The drive up the A96 clings in vain to my brain like my excrement sticks to my torso under the power of the shower jet. Both blasted away, I have another day to work through. And the clean and quiet stoma smiles up at me in its annoyingly rosy fresh state. Fuck you, Julian!

The Dr Jekyll and Mr Hyde of my body. Dr Jekyll

is forever suckering me in ... today is a new beginning, there, just there, and hey presto, I have affixed a brand-new bag. Completely sealed according to the good doctor. I must look the fool I feel as sometimes within minutes and often less than a couple of hours later there is no hiding from the reality of Mr Hyde.

And the stoma nurses have never known a case like mine. Or so I've been told, yet another good for nothing repetition. Do something, it's your job, think outside the bag. Thank you and goodnight, yet it's not even ten in the morning and it's going to be another long winter's day despite the shortage of light, both outside and within my own dimmed world.

The irony of feeling empowered by losing sight of my blue sky. Fuck off! And language comes into play as I now, once again fresh as a baby after a nappy change, await *next*. But I do not kid myself. Even though counting my blessings might seem foolish in the extreme it is what I do, what I have to do. I need to move this body and mind forward ... somehow. And I am blessed that I mostly have the inner wherewithal to do so. For *otherwise* doesn't bear thinking about for me.

My visiting missions, and I do still give myself the highfaluting title of having a parishioner role within my community circle, is to look for solutions. I have one of my shortest-lived bosses to thank for this outlook. One Ian Martin who I shared a birthday with. I don't think Tony was that taken with Ian Martin's style, or lack of it, but for me one sentence was enough, *come to me with solutions not problems*. I am probably paraphrasing. It was comforting that he could be approached with problems as long as one had the resolution in hand.

It is actually such a simple approach, though in the years since stated I have come to realise that it requires a certain mental disposition. Positivity. And goodness, at times I have lost that plot, and have needed Karen and Tony to steer me back to it, but some within my ken cannot make any move towards resolution. They are overwhelmed like a rabbit in full beam headlights. Not a state I recommend. Even without the Tony or the Karen slap I am very lucky to have the resource to pull up the Velcro boot straps.

Laugh, I almost have to; gallows, macabre, scatological … bring all the humour one can muster on, black on black, eh? Especially with these iron tablets. Okay, enough!

And the sun is actually shining on this particular day in March, not long until the clocks spring forward, an hour's less kip, an hour's less chance of a stoma bag leak ... see, such positivity. I am a card.

And how do you keep the card from going soggy, and my mind trips off on to stoma bag leaks again, and this from the man who claims his cup is brimming over with blessings. Oh indeed, and then I throw in my own reality check and, albeit momentarily, come up against a wall of doubt. A damp wad of papier-mâché has little impact against a solid edifice. And your point is?

The point is how easy it is to go off track, and end up in that cul-de-sac of despair, which is why it is important to be able to have the solution driven mindset. And, where possible and welcome to use it to assist others. Oh yes, not all want to be dragged out of their wallow. So be it. You are no-one's keeper but your own. Say your piece and know when to walk away, learn to not allow other's negativity to impinge upon your own good vibrations.

Oh, and here's another lesson that I have learnt during the stoma months. Another somewhat sad but true one, there are those who like to hear of your ill health, it makes them feel better to know that you are unwell. Now that's what I call taking up the fact that there are always people worse off than yourself far, far too close-up and personal. Yet, it is a need some have. To feel the comfort that your own distress gives them during or within their own arena of illness. Go figure. But it's true. And sadly, they tend not to realise. One friend I banned from hospital visits, for they thrived off news of friends' ill health. I am not making this up, honest, tell them you are fine and they will bemoan their own state of mediocre health, hip, eyesight, fatigue, but mention excessive bag leaks and they brighten up with dynamic interest. Details and more details.

*

I have to admit that during the initial COVID-19 months I was not the world's most ardent observer of hand washing. Isolation my excuse. I would leave the post where it fell through the letterbox for twenty-four hours before picking it up. I would wash my hands after the delivery of an online shopping order. Otherwise, it was restricted to after toilet visits and when visibly dirty from gardening. Mucky, grubby kid!

A right kick up the pants having a stoma proved to be for handwashing. I almost washed them raw, saved from that by the fact that I was not physically able to garden to my former capacity, so though they bled and I had to resort to E45 itch cream it was in its own way limited to the stoma bag's demands, be that either attending to leaks and thus bag changes, or to the emptying of its contents. Of perhaps no particular interest except to myself, the cracked skin was particularly thin and susceptible to bleed at the wrist joint wrinkles, in what seemed like to me spontaneous bleeding. I would suddenly notice a bloody stain on a worktop, a mug or an item of clothing and wonder where it was from – my wrists. Thankfully the cream was effective and eventually the issue faded as a concern. Yippee!

*

Trepidation defeated. I successfully negotiated the Texas concert that Paul and Louise had bought me for a pre-COVID birthday or

Christmas ages ago ... like I can remember which ... so much was cancelled ... one lost track of the reinstatement and the original reason. Well, I did. Stoma the excuse, acceptable or not. It was mine.

Ironically it was Louise who caught COVID after the event, so to speak ... then eventually Paul and it dripped down through their extended family.

Both Louise and Paul were amazed that I had escaped, again. I was on antibiotics at the time for the cyst on the left side of the base of my neck. Though I blamed the antibiotics for keeping me *dry* perhaps they were equally at fault for the fact that in this instance I avoided COVID.

And, yes, my sleepover was a success in being a leak-free dry one. Not without traumas, obviously – well I took a while to drop off, so concerned about bag security, and the placing of the rectangular bed pad just-so. As if that wasn't enough to occupy my mind of its multicoloured discharge scenarios I had been given away-at-college Olly's room and so had an Arsenal poster hanging like the sword of Damocles over my head – thankfully only in 2D.

The stuff of nightmares.

I had really enjoyed the concert, so cleverly devised and performed in two distinct halves, almost by two distinct bands … an acoustic first set from the twentieth century era and a rocky twenty-first century second half. Loving Sharleen's voice, if not her language so much. Old? Unwell? If an excuse is needed for such a view. And the three of us were full of it on the drive back from Southend.

I was hungry, but knew better. I had munched my way through a cheese sandwich on the way to the concert; not that easy to achieve crumb free in the dark within a moving car, before adding my manual dexterity issues, despite cutting the sandwich into allegedly my grip-friendly pieces. A plain cheese sandwich on white bread was my staple *going out* meal, it was as fool proof as was possible with my stoma. This was by no means empirical, but it was as close as I could get to a comfort zone. Sad but true.

And such a successful outing as this turned out

to be was vital in the general state of stoma bag play psyche. However much fear fringed the whole experience, I know Louise and Paul would have understood if I had drowned Olly's mattress and I know I would have bought a replacement one if I had. I know. Likewise, if I had soiled Paul's upholstered car seats …

Joy! None of this occurred. I had as good a time as was possible with my combined physical and mental state. Giving the needed illusion that I wasn't sealed within one of my own stoma bags.

I know, obviously I jest as they don't fucking seal, do they? Well, not against my body, that's for sure. Now body shape, there's another issue. And I want to say adieu to the stoma nurses, but this was another area where we had different thoughts, perspectives. They had theory, I had reality. They wanted me to put their theory into practice, whilst practice made a mockery of their theory. My body shape post-ileostomy meant that the majority of my night time leaks occurred in a direct line to my navel, and latterly the subtle (okay, sneaky) day time leaks occurred at the lowest edge of the bag. Gravity? A smidge, but more likely due to the contour cavity that had been chiselled out below the stoma. My body shape did not fit the stoma nurses' ideal. Ladies, please, it did not shape up to my ideal either – but it was my reality and as such was theirs too. Their denial was somewhat less than helpful. This is a tongue-in-cheek under-statement. (Yes, I do feel that strongly about it.) In fact, I shall remove my brackets. Yes, I do feel that strongly about it.

And where's the dietician?

April 2022

Is the mike off … can I swear now?

Disabled sense of humour.

Removing eggs from carton. The latter a fresh reminder of the degeneration of my manual dexterity. Suddenly, one day, lo and behold, extracting the first egg from a six pack has become a challenge. The finger grip to be just so, if too light or two tight the digits will slip off of the oval. Shock, horror, if said eggs aren't at their freshest the shells might even crack under the force of the attempted extraction. But don't tell Sue G, she'd freak out at my flagrant disregard for use-by dates. And there is, are even, solutions you can work around, though you persevere at proving how difficult it is to extract that first egg. How high can the challenge bar get?

Hey, focus, dealing with stoma bag leaks is enough for now. Forever! How long is forever? This sort of self-teasing is doing the total opposite of lightening your spirits.

It won't be forever, not your forever. Not mine. Just seems … and you are like a child dealing with how far away tomorrow is from now. Grow-up! Yes, tell yourself – act both parts … no-one will hear, or wet themselves at your ridiculousness. No tears now, this will pass, it all passes and you have to gird your loins and stoma bag. That's better, ridiculousness in a gallows humour sense, but at least it is humour. And that's how it goes. Day to day, yes *dear inner child*, tomorrow comes.

Lunchtime also comes around and the cat and I share a ham sandwich on white. When I say share, the cat has the ham and I have the white bread. Deal? The cat approves, so there you go, happiness spread like butter stored outside the confines of the fridge. Easily! Some days, despite your best efforts you fritter away the minutes and then hours, knowing you are doing it almost exacerbates the doing, like a tooth cavity that your tongue cannot resist finding. Vacant, and it's definitely not pretty, a metaphorical slap is but that. Like today, it will pass, but for now it lingers on, and on. Knowing that tomorrow you will wake up energised is a lie that you are more than happy to swallow as you wallow on the afternoon's tide of complete indifference. Any thoughts revolve solely around the current stoma bag and the extent of it being leak proof. Extent as in length of time.

All is time driven.

*

There, I had done it. It was what I wanted. Next …

On the 4th of April, 2022, and I had officially gone private, seeing Mary-Jane at the Sloane Hospital in Beckenham. In her own way, bless her, she was sort of apologetic for the fact that she could not operate on me through the NHS. Sort of, for she wasn't really an apologise type person. Calling me Andrew for instance instead of Neil was obviously my fault for being called Neil Andrews, not hers, nor the speed with which she felt the need to do things at.

Anyway, she advised it would be London Bridge that she would have me admitted to, not the Sloane, nor Chelsfield Park, due to the extent of the procedure and the potential need for after-care. After life?

(Again, I would trip ... after life, before life, renewed life, life itself?)

*

To be fair, in my last real interfacing with them, the stoma nurses did try and fight my corner. I have, I know, gone on at length about the liquidity of my discharge. A theme of this tale! So, better late than never, really(!!!!), they proffer a solution. We are in April mind, and I have had a stoma for over six months.

Absorb - odour neutralising absorbent gel- Box of 150 x 3g Sachets - Code PFW6.

Well; I never! Obvious, isn't it?

These little sachets of crystals absorb the liquid discharge and expand, thus thickening my discharge, hopefully making leakages less likely. That's the idea anyway. But guess what occurs when I decide that they do add positive value to my life with a stoma?

> Are you, i.e. the PRUH, able to supply me with anymore as the surgery pharmacy has just phoned and suggested I try you as they are not considered vital within the south-east region for stoma care so cannot be prescribed? I did explain how VITAL they were to my stoma care!

Yes, you have read it right. The prescription was turned down. Thankfully, in this instance, the stoma nurses were able, and did, come to my rescue.

*

Easter Sunday, and as so often, Karen had invited me over to share her and Kevin's family Easter lunch. Years and years of inclusivity, though this year I shouldn't have gone, I shouldn't even have set off, but I had agreed, gratefully as well as willingly, and I am not one to let people down. I definitely try not to.

But there's brave faces and then sheer stupidity. The trouble is with something like a stoma and its unpredictability your decision making is almost a double-bluff of what is real as well as what is likely to happen next. Next? Like a lemon, I sat on their sun-kissed patio sipping a tumbler of water desperately trying not to show any sort of pained look.

I had stomach cramps, the worst since my New Year escapade that had ended with me overnighting in A&E. Wasn't the whole point of the ileostomy to eradicate such pain seizures. Give me a break. Please! Pretty, please.

Kevin was an excellent cook, as well as a masterly calm chef, he was catering for twelve, luckily no-one (yours truly excepted) had food fads to talk of.

Oh! dear Neil! Now you are dismissing the allergies and such of others as mere fads. Since when did you become so intolerant? *Today!* I silently cry, in self-defence, as I try not to double up in pain. I need to leave. I know Kevin and

Karen will understand. Their son-in-law will demolish my helping, no waste. I discard that thought, my concern is more on how to depart without making it a scene … preferably unseen. Likely it would have to be a quiet word with but one of the pair. Talking to them both simultaneously would create a moment. Karen smiled as she walked by me on her way to the kitchen escorted by her granddaughter. Now or never. I fell in behind as she teased out a to-hand wet-wipe to clean Connie's sticky fingers for her. I would have felt a tad of envy if my stomach had not seized control of my attention at that very moment.

No, I would not accept the offer of a bed to sleep it off. I was still all too aware of leaks and more leaks. Yes, of course I would WhatsApp as soon as I reached home. Wretched home … as I felt an involuntary dry spasm catch the back of my throat.

Gizzy fed it was straight to bed and into the psychological comfort of the foetal position, even if it did not translate into physical comfort. The spasms built and racked my body, I yelped and

moaned, *no one heard at all, not even the chair[4]*
… and I thought 'you are funny Karen!' any
attempt, any, to take my mind off the inner
process. Realising it is a process and that it
needs to work through my core does not really
help. Not really. Oh, I can tell you why alright.
It's because I never, ever, know when I have
reached rock bottom, or the peak, depending on
the inverse view of my universe. So, I scrunch
up, and attempt to scrunch up even more.

These moments always serve as reminders to
myself why I have never felt the need for
recreational drugs … let alone morphine … for I
have seen through Huxley's doors through
stomach cramps. No Karen, I am not funny. I
am in agony and thought the whole point of the
stoma was that these cramps would no longer
occur.

Right on cue, its own cue, my bag started to fill
during the course of the night, as I had collapsed
into sleep. As ever, the day after the day before
I am as weak as my own extensive watery
discharge as I fill my bag … thankfully not to
leaking point … although my *Stoma Diaries*

---

[4] I am … I said – Neil Diamond.

described it as a deluge. Punch drunk, where my stomach feels like it would if it had been kicked by a horse. Perhaps I should take recreational drugs so as to come up with more original phrases. For sure, I don't think I would actually survive being kicked by a horse.

Karen, help!

And the earliest Mary-Jane could operate was the Saturday of the Jubilee weekend? Wisely, I didn't hold my breath. As expected, it was, within forty-eight hours amended to the Saturday after – the 11th. All systems go!

Well, I was discharging liquid like there was no tomorrow today. Right now. Joy! And my weight had dropped to below sixty-four kilos. I was that concerned that I actually raised the issue about weight-loss and whether there was a weight below which Mary-Jane wouldn't operate. It would appear not, was the answer – which I actually didn't find reassuring … *you takes my money and I have no choice*. You gotta laugh. Perhaps.

Anyway, we now can move forward emotionally. But not physically as the stoma and its bag are still revolting. For days after the Easter Sunday cramps, I produce litres of liquid. It's where I really want the appliance of science. Tell me why? Why does a poached salmon steak and plain penne produce so much liquid on one day and remain idle until a firmer substance is released on another? It's where the bottom line has to be that no-one actually knows what my insides are up to. And as long as I am not experiencing death throes no-one cares enough. As the stoma nurses have already stated they have never come across a case like mine. Such continued comfort NOT.

But, comfort yourself my man, the clock is ticking … and not just in some NHS fantasy world, but in your own real world of pounds, shillings and pence. (Sometimes it's good to show one's age.)

Excerpt from my email to the stoma nurses on the 27th …

> I am having a bit of a bad time at the moment. I haven't (had to) take any loperamide for over 24 hours as since lunch yesterday I have had awful stomach cramps with very little discharge (other than, eventually, wind) … this particular

> attack has been building since the Easter weekend. I had nothing to eat after lunch yesterday but have had breakfast and lunch and think lunch is trying to exit!

Bless them! They were sorry to hear that I was unwell, but their bottom-line solution always ended up with me going to A&E. Well, it would. Just in case.

And, I was to let them know how I was. So, I did …

> I was dry retching, and strangely enough did a large number two out of my bottom today. Very weird. The light headedness has been back for about ten days which I put down to the continuous descent in weight. Will see how overnight/tomorrow goes ref A&E.

I didn't go to A&E and what I took to be my current equilibrium returned as we traipsed into May.

The bottom, as opposed to stoma, poo was the second since my 6th October operation, the first also exiting after severe stomach cramping back in October. Were these carbonised rocks wind-stoppers? But wind was generally exiting through my stoma, thus my use of the wind release valves.

Wind release valves! I had to laugh, really and truly, that or cry. I think I have, once or twice, mentioned wind and its filling of my stoma bag to the point where I think it will detach itself from my body if it hasn't already started to, to find the bag is empty of visible content but merely full of wind. Online I go and discover that there are *wind release valves* on the stoma supplies market. Thank you, no thank you stoma nurses … another on the need-to-know basis. And sort of bypassing the stoma nurses need to take action I note that they can be ordered from off the Fittleworth site. Yes, it will be viewed by said nurses and need the GP's sign-off, but worth it. And they are signed off and though I may be approaching the stoma bag end game they do prove to be a very useful accoutrement. You pierce a hole into your stoma bag as near the top as possible and then affix the sticky backed valve around the small hole and as and when open the valve to dispense the dry wind that emanates from the stoma. I tended to leave the valve open all day and night. The exception being when in company.

So, had this particular stomach cramp wind been lurking inside since the pre-October op? See, this is exactly the sort of question no-one could answer.

Such a bummer being unique, man.

*

Solace. And sometimes, the need to escape one's immediate surroundings. I have my own not-so-secret place, the gardens at Great Comp, discovered by chance one day whilst browsing through The Garden, the monthly RHS magazine. Too much information, maybe, but the initial visits were FREE as RHS members gain access without payment in the autumn. But I immediately fell in love with the place, subsequently becoming a season ticket holder, so that whenever the mood strikes or the need arises solace is basically thirty minutes away.

It is magical in a number of ways, key for me when wanting to escape is the space. And even with a seemingly full car park the gardens seem either empty or the others on paths you cross appear to respect each other's aura and will exchange contented smiles or a softly spoken pleasantry. Otherwise, you are lost in a lush green world where birdsong accompanies you, be it a blackbird singing its heart out as though busking at a tube station or jackdaws in avid conversation, all seeming to speak at once as though at a meeting where the chairman has lost control. Near the staff room there are bird feeders, apart from blue and great there are long-tailed tits in their mini-flocks, chaffinches and I am sure other species should one choose to linger.

Apart from space and flat walks and camellias and magnolias the gardens are known for housing Dyson's Nurseries' salvia collection, with at most times of the year good value plants to purchase. It is where I fell for the salvia guaranitica family, for me it's a love of brushing against the sage laden scent of the plants as well as the majesty of named varieties like *super trouper*. (I wonder if named by an ABBA fan?) Previously I had somewhat despised the salvia family, for in my limited experience they were but the dark, small, almost insignificant garden annual that lacked vibrancy. I do like a vibrant garden! Great Comp opened my eyes to what the salvia world has to offer. Again, being me and pernickety, *hot lips* was okay in other folk's gardens but not mine. Though I do like some of the mono-coloured shrub varieties it is the herbaceous that catch my eye and my different coloured pound notes or credit card. *Pink pong* the favourite out of all these, for it not only appears the hardiest but is also easiest to take cuttings from.

What a surprise, I have digressed.

Great Comp is not huge by any stretch of the imagination, being but seven acres big, but it packs a punch with its various constituent parts, and although regulars may find the newly installed signs somewhat over the top it must be useful for both the first time as well as the irregular visitor. The bambooserie is not my favourite section but is definitely my favourite word. I think, for similar phonic reasons I bought my first *pink pong* salvia, for at the time I hadn't seen them in flower at Great Comp let alone in my own garden.

And again, a digression, at least based on the same plant.

As the garden opens at the end of spring the snowdrop family are the first to flourish with the camelia, rhododendron and magnolia looking magnificent for months rather than weeks, with an under covering of stupendous hellebores. The paths that house these overhanging vistas are down the left-hand side as you enter the magical garden, marking the border. The view then opens up, as one follows the path around, after fresh hellebore and camelia planting one walks along a path where soon to flower perennial pink geranium grow, amidst generally smaller azaleas and camelias, with some viburnum snowball showing off their pompoms of white flowers.

This path leads to the temple. The temple is one of many of the odd bits and pieces, ruins or follies, that are found around the garden that make it such an ideal place for parents and grandparents both to take the pre-school toddlers. An enchanting garden for imaginations to run beautifully wild.

The path back from the temple leads to an expanse of lawn that has an azalea border that dazzles in April with red and orange hues, and further around this stretch of lawn there is a magnificent late summer through to autumn show of rudbeckia, dahlias and marigolds. Grasses and salvia abound here too, as do some magnificent hydrangea specimens. The back of the Great Comp house looks out onto a lawn that has a resplendent herbaceous border, walled to right and left, that not only contains salvia of a wide-ranging size and hue, but also a great palette of other herbaceous favourites. Near the moon arch that leads to the tea-room thalictrum abound, as is their want.

Through the arch there are to your left verdant alcoves for those who wish a more secluded cuppa, whilst to your right is the open seating area, with a huge magnolia as canopy, as well as the tea-room itself. As well as cake! For those making more of a meal of their outing, tasty lunches can be purchased.

And finally, I dare you to pass the exit without being tempted to purchase your own salvia memento of your visit. A bit of an issue if you have a season ticket and regularly use it.

Solace achieved. Equilibrium reset. I am a firm believer in the importance of serenity in the maintenance good health. The finding of seemingly innocuous tasks that give you that feeling of inner peace and reduce both real and imagined stress. Gardening gives me that. Oh, I know, it can at times be a frustrating pastime but on the whole if exudes a feel-goodness that knocks any negativity on the head. The continuity or the lack of ever finishing is one of its potentially perverse joys, take deadheading cosmos, during the season a never-ending task, but most rewarding as the blooms keeps on flowering, their reward for your attentive labours. Pottering! Is it possible to beat this catch all, little insignificant tasks that all add up during the course of the garden meander … a weed here, a snip of a branch there, a tie-back over there, a snail placed mid lawn … is the latter action crueller than a swift despatch? Not rhetorical, I honestly don't know. What I do know is that I have an awful lot of snails and they appear to enjoy laying their eggs in flower pots that house my baby plants, an on-tap food supply.

So, as I battle my way back to what I call good health I work on this appreciation of the now, the being, the existing. Does it sound all too fey? Hey, when you've been where I've been over these last twelve months it's all out there as unreal. Grab what you can to hold on to as reality.

But don't get me wrong, all this positivity isn't as easy as I wish it was. I have to work at it, to maintain the *blue sky* as my compass point, my mantra. Smile you're on Candid Camera, even if the camera in question is your own reflection in the tooth-brushing mirror or the car's rear view one, or the one in your mind's eye … the ever-present Big Brother.

But it's what's needed, maintaining focus and attitude, and why being discharged from hospital as early as possible is so important to one's mental welfare as well as physical. A fact that I don't think is given as much credence as it deserves. Trust me, it is a vital component of well-being.

Sometimes, yes sometimes, even I can be hit with the apathy stick, and when it happens it cannot be laid at the door of anaemia. Even I know the difference between tiredness and what the fuck. My apathy targets the repetitive human tasks, even with labour saving devices like washing machines and dishwashers, oh yes, the mere loading and unloading all seems so pointless and I feel but like a somewhat aged hamster, making its wheel go round and around without actually getting anywhere itself. Do you know what I mean? Buying porridge oats and milk, buying porridge oats and milk, buying porridge oats and milk. Can it be diminished? Seeking a purpose, a sense. Is the futility the result of living on your own? Is it the lack of faith in the hereafter? Too much time contemplating one's navel? I would suggest *no* to the latter question, for it is by no means original thought, and it is not merely a post-op syndrome, it has been there or thereabouts in many guises throughout this existence.

Take shaving. Why? You'll just have to do it again the next day. Is that why when *clean shaven* in my working life I shaved the night before and didn't bother on a Thursday night, and the reason why I so often had a beard? But even a beard has to be *kept* – trimmed and the neck shaved. No? Yes ... except ... so during COVID I just let it grow, from day one of lockdown until barbers were given sanction to re-open. I became a Victorian grandpapa. Suddenly I regained hair on the top of my head, not a side effect of COVID, for I hadn't had it by then. How did that happen? Twenty-five years of a number one cut, and you forget. There's another of those repetitions.

When non-iron shirts appeared, I took it literally and did not iron them, purely based on their selling point, not on their post wash-and-dry look. They are non-iron so you don't iron them. One less turn, of the hamster wheel. But I won't labour the point … being a minimalist ironer, who irons socks and hankies nowadays. Who uses handkerchiefs nowadays. A tissue, a tissue, all fall down …

Another of my self-cons is that I do no cleaning. Well, for goodness' sake, why employ a lady-who-does, oops sorry, a person-who-does, if you are going to end up doing it yourself? It's bad enough the tidying up before the person arrives. I kid you not. (And I have told a bit of a white lie, for I do on occasion get the vacuum cleaner out if I have scheduled visitors during said person's holiday … for even a hamster has standards. Though my propensity is to avoid home entertaining during their three weeks of missed cleans.)

So, to ponder, and I am already feeling better when I consider growing annuals, such as cosmos. Yes, the thoughts of pointless repetition are still there, but somehow or something within my being moves on and away from this sloth inducing what's-the-point take on the sowing, pricking out, potting on, distribution to friends' process. Why?

May 2022

3rd May, 2022.

Ms Mary-Jane,
Consultant Colorectal &
Laparoscopic Surgeon,
BMI Sloane.

By email.

Dear Ms Mary-Jane,

Neil Andrews

I hope this finds you well.

I have some questions with regards to my 11th June operation. Since we spoke on the 21st April, I have had no communication from the London Bridge hospital. When should I start to hear from them and the anaesthetist etc.?

Whilst I appreciate that answers to some of the below depend on how the operation goes a rough guide would be useful:

1. Percentage chance of waking from the operation to find I still have a stoma?
2. Should an emergency occur during the op do I get transferred to Guy's?
3. All being well length of stay in hospital?
4. All being well length of time once discharged I should have someone overnight with me?
5. Post operation dietary requirements? Will I be given a recovery programme to follow?

6. Is post-op care NHS? Do I go to the PRUH A&E with constipation or diarrhoea issues post discharge?
7. Full (in my terms) recovery timeframe?

On a separate but related note I have not felt that well since before Easter, with two severe bouts of stomach cramps. The PRUH stoma nurses advised A&E attendance if the symptoms persisted. Is the current level of discomfort, with trapped wind, something I just have to live with going forward, even post reversal?

My weight loss is, it seems, purely a personal concern. However, in trying to stem this and eating more I am convincing myself that the pains of late are due to a new intestinal blockage ... this is purely in my mind, right? At now 62.85 kgs is there a point at which I am too light to operate on? My surgery pharmacist has switched me from Fortisip drinks to Aymes shakes, the former tended to flush through with no benefit. Five days in it is too early to state whether the shakes will redress the weight loss issue.

I look forward to hearing from you in due course.

Yours,

*

May, the complete month to leak through before the reversal, but still all hands to the pumps, aka the stoma bags! The beginning of May and suddenly my stoma had, virtually overnight, doubled in size. Again, *this happens* was as clinical as the stoma nurses were able to be. Shit happens! And it did, but now I had an over large stoma dribbling blood when I showered.

Press the panic button? There is no panic button, *this happens* ... and, it's not a Christmas cracker motto ... oh flippancy begone. I jest, stay, oh please stay. Dearest Sanity!

Oh, and have I mentioned my toes in this tome

yet? My big toes were for years my Achilles' heel. Eventually, obviously, now replaced by my gut. Displaced they decided that they would rebel, so the left big toe had a burgeoning ulcer that needed a dressing kept on for a week. I am, sort of, laughing as I type … it's the recall, and the getting through … though at the time.

The stoma nurses had come up trumps with the provision of the crystal sachets that my GP practice said that their parent health board would no longer support prescriptions for. Thank you, sarcastically to the health board but genuinely to the stoma nurses, for the amount of liquid I was currently discharging at night desperately needed the crystal sachets as a thickening agent. I used six sachets in one night alone, two per each fresh bag as I tried to stem the liquid flow from leaking.

I also, quite unbelievably, had to do battle (ish) with the surgery over the need for stoma bags that would fit over the enlarged stoma. Though I had a few left-over of the first ever batch with the original discharge aperture, my main supply was now a trim fit for the stoma that had shrunk over winter. If your stoma bag was a loose fit then this exacerbated skin burns and blistering from the excrement that the stoma ideally emptied directly into the snug fitting bag. (I know you required repeated clarification on this.)

The supply of the accoutrements to life with a stoma generally worked as follows. I went on to the Fittleworth website and ordered what I needed. Fittleworth being, I assumed, either the NHS supplier of choice, or the PRUH's or perhaps even that of the south-east region. I didn't really need to know, or care. Sort of. Back in the beginning, there was Adam and Eve and a fig leaf, but from the 6th of October I had a stoma bag and a small vanity-sized bag for stoma related items (sprays, creams, wipes) emblazoned with *Fittleworth*. Come to think of it, I don't think it was until my one and only home visit from the stoma nurses that I was advised about how to access supplies. Through the Fittleworth website. A website that was not particularly friendly let alone intuitive. In frustration I would on occasion give up and ask the stoma nurses how to locate certain products on the website.

Anyway, having registered as a client they would then confirm my order and process it with an expected delivery date. But I noticed, quite early on that there tended to be a fair amount of slippage in expected with actual delivery dates. Their call pick up was also quite poor and initially emails went unanswered. The stoma nurses then put a supervisor on to my case and there was an improvement, though there remained a frustrating inconsistency.

> *We will also pass your contact information over to Alice who is the Fittleworth representative who can get in touch to try and smooth things out and see where the holdup is coming from.*

Now in this emergency scenario caused by the enlarged stoma Fittleworth were asking for my assistance in ensuring the doctor's surgery signed off on my request. So, it seems, I put in a prescription request to Fittleworth, who then forwarded it for sign off to my doctor. (I believe via the PRUH stoma nurses, though I was never able to ascertain this one hundred percent.) When I contacted the surgery, they of course blamed Fittleworth for lack of clarity. I wasn't asking for anyone to be blamed. Just provide me with the fucking bags. I was even considering discharging my leaking bags on the surgery doorstep in frustration at the red tape. Clarity? How did this request for stoma bags suddenly require a clarity than one assumes had been missing from previous orders. Please!

Thankfully the stoma nurses were able to plug the hole of this particular emergency.

> *Will 11AM be too early to collect the intermediate bags tomorrow?*

My email to them read …

> Much needed. Since my email to the surgery, I have spoken to both them and Fittleworth. The surgery blaming Fittleworth's unclear prescription orders! Upshot, surgery promises to sign off today and Fittleworth will expedite one box prior to receiving full prescription sign off.

Result.

> *I have left the pouches for you to collect at the main reception.*

> *Best wishes,*

> *Stoma Nurse A*

Clinical Nurse Specialist, Stoma Care.

STOP RIGHT THERE – specialist and care! Permission to take issue with?

This, on the 11th of May was the last email contact with the stoma nurses, with the reversal scheduled to take place in a month to the day's time.

Thoughts? A and B were pleasant people who obviously found my issues if not me myself a bit of an unknown. Personally I found that their statement that they had never come across someone before with the leakage issues and diet issues that I had as a somewhat irrelevant stand-alone statement, for surely it should have been accompanied by a *let's get to the bottom of this together* attitude, whereas I was fed repetition upon repletion of the diet sheet I was already using whilst they threw marshmallows and jelly babies into the mix ... the latter proving to be a recipe for flooding the stoma and soaking me and my surroundings. I was, I admit, a bit heavy handed at times, especially when enquiring about duty of care. They seemed to have no sense of urgency, let alone responsibility, when it came to trying to find a dietician. Only I (and my friends) seemed duly concerned about my weight loss. With a stoma resulting from an ileostomy how much goodness is retained from food intake? I was eating a lot of salmon, trout and chicken, backed up with pasta.

When the next lot of sending-me-to-bed cramps hit at the end of May I didn't even bother contacting them, litres of subsequent watery discharge regardless. I had come, it seems, to accept what they could and couldn't add to easing my life with a stoma.

A thank you though, to them, for initially giving me the belief that I could cope with the manual dexterity of stoma bag application. It's just such a shame that they omitted so much ... from beginning to end.

*

Then there's the cat, Gizzy.

Moving on to the next incident ...

Only days, a lot of days later did I even thinking of connecting two with two to make four ... even this required visual confirmation ... which I duly got.

Gizzy was a catcher of squirrels, however the season was usually October, when they appeared the most distracted hiding their nuts. But this was early May. I assumed an ailing squirrel or one distracted out of squirrel-catching season. A dead one whatever the cause. Of its capture.

Out! Out! Out! The cry Gizzy was used to hearing when his ungrateful owner declined his gifts. But I did open the door for Gizzy, so he didn't need to drag his catch back out through the cat flap from whence he had come. Helpful me. In my anthropomorphic view he toddled off somewhat disconsolate that his generosity of spirit was not appreciated. Right!

Out of sight out of mind. And give me a break folks, I was somewhat preoccupied.

And in my mind as days followed days, I assumed my stoma bag contents must have had a greater whiff than previously, or so my nose assumed. Was this the downside of my wind releasing valves? The stoma issues were such an integral part of my twenty-four-hour cycle, yes, a day, that the pong was but another reason why the reversal couldn't come quick enough. And it wasn't.

I opened the bathroom window to try and dissipate the odour, and told myself that it worked, which it did … eventually.

Although I know that come May my butter dish should reside in the fridge and only make an appearance thirty to sixty minutes before need, I do tend to leave it out all year, such the speed with which I go through butter anyway. And the point is?

Patience! If I bloody have it surely you can oblige me with a modicum?

What was that on the butter dish lip? A tiny café-au-lait speck, was it moving? It was, it was a minuscule maggot. I must have brought it in from gardening. Not that I'd done it before, but I did tend to drag leaves and dirt indoors, admittedly more on my boots than anything else. But this wriggling worm could have attached itself to me as I brushed by some shrubbery foliage.

Get this! Being me, it isn't a case of zapping, i.e.,

Stoma in a teacup

killing the grub, oh no I place it in the *to be composted* bowl, along with the tea bags. Give it a chance. Chance to become what?

So, when over the next day or two I notice a further couple or so of self-same maggots on the kitchen worktop I start to wonder, and literally turn my gaze upwards. Directly above the peninsular work surface was nothing but the kitchen ceiling and one of the nine embedded lights. Five, above the sink area worked off one switch, with a separate switch for the remaining four that lit the rest of the room.

(Don't EVER choose this sort of lighting ... however much your electrician, builder, friend, Geoff might recommend them. Have you ever tried to change the bulbs? With AMC? Be my guest! And as for them blowing something if not fuses ... most of the ones upstairs no longer work ... I digress. But please take heed.)

The light-fitting I am looking up at isn't exactly a snug fit, the bulb has obviously been changed at some point and in the process the casing has not been returned to its original position. Ho hum! *C'est la vie!*

I can only think, as oppose to blame, that my stoma-fixated life had me less curious … initially. And after the initially phase had passed it was my builder friend.

Geoff, said builder friend, was out and I declined to leave a voicemail …

> Geoff it's Neil, could maggots be falling from through the kitchen ceiling light-fitting?

They're coming to take me away, ha-ha, he-he!

But they were. Spock logic would so advise the Trekkies. And I had to believe it. The impossibility dawning on me as I ventured upstairs. *Ventured* for I rarely left my ground floor life, there being no need. Perhaps I exaggerate with *rarely* as the chosen word. Infrequently might be more appropriate; only-if-necessary, would be precise.

This planned climb was an adventure into the unknown, except for the dread that I did know what I would find. I could not actually recall how many weeks it had been since I last needed anything from upstairs. Months? And as you may recall. Reggie is only required to clean

Stoma in a teacup

upstairs before Karen, or Karen and Kevin, arrive for a sleepover visit.

I now climb steps and stairs one at a time, right foot followed by the left onto step one, right foot followed by the left onto step two ... and we arrive in my own time. And I do own time.

It was not a pretty sight. I hadn't actually expected this, as such. Expectations? Dread? Telling myself this would not be what I would find.

A desiccated squirrel! Flat as a pancake, almost. As if a taxidermist worked in 2D as opposed to 3D. Thankfully the smell that I had believed had emanated from me had gone, been eaten away ...

But the mess and underlying gore ... one of Gizzy's predecessors had had toileting issues and the carpet in the area already had *cleaned* stains ... welcome to an additional one. I must admit that in the past I have put Gizzy's predecessors' gifts in the food-waste bins. A practice I followed with Gizzy's squirrels. Well, technically it is food waste, we have nicked the cat's food, thus creating waste. Technically! But, back to the clean up or the newest cleaned stain on the upstairs' landing carpet. Under the dehydrated corpse was a bloody wriggling mess. Oh yes – maggots. Maggots just waiting to wrestle through the carpet and floorboard and light fitting onto the kitchen worktop. Sweet!

The remains of the squirrel did remind me of the roadrunner Merry Melodies cartoon, beep-beep! This fur covered cardboard-like shape ended up in one of the compost bins. I grinned as I did so, for what would *Airplane* fans make of that? A flattened Davey Crockett hat? A brooch? I digress into flippant mode. Back indoors, with dustpan and brush I attempted to sweep up the larva and pupa that had lain under the animal. Yes, dull bronze pupae aplenty. This load was deposited below the bird feeder. The circle of life.

For sure, I was being given plenty of step exercise today as next I started on the process of addressing the colour of the bloodstained carpet. *What a mess!* I kept vocalising. I assume by way of encouragement as well as, I am sure, awe. The second day of cleaning I bought a patent Dr. Beckmann product to aid my elbow grease. And my mind. I now declared it a cleaned stain. One that Reggie would not have

Stoma in a teacup

to face. I was good that way. Stoma spray, cat vomit, spilled wine. Yes, it's true, I was one of the millions who tidy-up before the cleaner arrives. Thankfully, nowadays, the cleaning of the upstairs is on a request basis. I would be able to work on further cleaning my cleaned stain before Reggie had any need to spot its existence, and perhaps unnecessarily enquire.

They think it's all over? I did. But for days, and I mean days, maggots and cocoons continued to surface through the pile. The carpet had developed into a science fiction nightmare. Give it time Neil. There was now nothing for the larva to eat once maggots, so I swept and fed the birds. Retrospectively I did ponder on whether seepage was still feeding hatched eggs. Dr Beckmann was a cleaning agent not a poison. Time. Patience.

And yes, maggots no longer dropped from my ceiling. The carpet no longer gave forth life. I went *phew!*

They think it's all over; I've heard say. And I now had other things on my mind. My reversal operation was but a week away. Yikes!

281

Whatever next? Flies, and more flies, that was what was next. Try saying that at speed with a mouthful of teeth.

At first, I stupidly thought mild weather, the attraction of Gizzy's unfinished breakfast. That's if I actually gave it a thought. Can I be blamed? The reversal was looming if not actually glooming ahead of me. Flies, a plague of flies was not a portent conducive to positive thinking.

Where were they coming from, and seemingly at set times of the day. There would be none around in the morning ... but by early afternoon it was to my exaggerated mindscape something akin to Hitchcock's *The Birds*, leaving Daphne du Maurier aside, with me opening the kitchen windows and door to assist the lazy flyers' exit. Like with the maggots I wasn't going to go out of my way to kill. Just buzz off, pretty please!

I went upstairs to check whether they were rising out of the carpet. What did I know after the larva experience? Yes, there were a couple of dead flies but not the number that appeared day after day in the kitchen, even after I put Gizzy's food dish away between his snacking visits.

Eventually I had to admit, with a shudder, that they must be entering the kitchen the same way as the maggots had, by means of the ceiling light-fitting. Really? Yes, really. What other explanation was there?

With now less than a week to my scheduled reversal operation I started to panic as to what to say to Ann-Marie about the fly infestation she would discover upon her Gizzy-feeding visits. My house was clean for goodness' sake. I really couldn't go into a longwinded explanation, however much veracity it had. Could I? No! Our communication was not of that sort. I needed to solve this before the Saturday.

Solve Neil?

Time! Time did come to mind, for the issue must be finite … I had done what I could to create an end game. Hadn't I? The life cycle of egg, larva, pupa, fly could not continue without a food source … so my thoughts went as I tried to swat the flies out the kitchen door, again.

The plague may have peaked on the Wednesday, by when I had decided on what information I would leave Ann-Marie with.

> If the fly problem persists, I shall
> deal with it upon my return having
> now unearthed the source ... I
> think.

I think! Wishful thinking pertaining to which part. Go away! Issue, go away. I strongly felt my mind needed to be solely focused on my health, on coming through the other side of Saturday. Not on flies.

I even asked Karen and Kevin who had kindly offered to deliver me to the hospital whether they could bring along a can of the strongest fly spray Kevin could lay his hands on, without elaborating. I really couldn't bring myself to discuss what was going on.

I had allowed it to become a private nightmare scene of *Poltergeist* proportions. Unclean! Up the stairs I went. All this exercise must be doing me good, upbeat. A few additions to the previously retrieved deceased flies, but again not the quantity that invaded the kitchen. I opened the nearest eave store cupboard, yes, some flies buzzed by me, and there were some empty husks. Like this one that lived on his own. Stop it!

Had I the right to be hopeful? Had the last reverberation of Gizzy's squirrel gift about played out? Though I didn't change the wording on my note to Ann-Marie I thought I felt a tad more optimistic by the end of fly-time that June Friday. Definitely a noticeable reduction … and although Karen and Kevin arrived *sans* fly spray my focus was now elsewhere.

June 2022

Even in the world of private medicine the occasional mistake is made. Stands back in flippant amazement. Surely not! Surely yes. Within a couple of days of being told that my reversal would occur on June 4th it was rearranged for the following Saturday, so as not to clash with the Jubilee four-day weekend. Expediency or cost? Would the cost of staff pay not have been passed on?

What's another week between stoma bags? Quite a bit as it transpires; my last diary entry of the 7th June reads …

4 Imodium at 22:35, after a shower
of shit, and shower.

All being well, fingers crossed, and wasn't this what I was after, I would definitely not be missing these scenes that could be straight out of *Poltergeist* or some such film. The flies, the shit, the whole script …

I had totally and utterly reached the point of not caring whether I came out the other side. Not in a wishing death upon myself sense but in a not wanting to have to deal with an existence of stoma bags and the physical and mental restrictions the eight months had imposed. I do, honestly, I do realise that eight months out of sixty-eight years is a tiny fraction, in fact less than one percent of my life.

Avoiding COVID-19 became the main distraction during the fortnight before the due date; Karen and Kevin erred very much on the side of caution whilst Tony and Sue G were a tad more casual. For myself, I was generally cool, calm and collected as long as it was outside.

Occupational therapy, of my own design, meant I was delivering plants that I *sold* for donations to the local hospice on the day before the endgame. I also changed my will and drove round to Mikhail and Elizabeth on that Friday, for them to witness my signature ... all of us signing the document as it rested on the top of their car; dropping plants off at customers along the way, as well as on the way home. My will had not been amended for nine years, not since the demise of my mother's sisters and whilst bequests to nephews and nieces required an inflation adjustment, so did the main beneficiary.

Adrenalin must have been coursing through my body as I reversed my car straight into the trunk of the tree on the pavement outside their home. BANG! Thankfully, it was *straight* into the tree, as I could not believe that it had escaped unscathed. Both in fact. Car and tree! An omen?

COVID-19 regardless I had travelled up to the London Bridge hospital by train for my pre-op assessment. Well, it was but one stop on the train. And, I really could not believe this, as all the hospital literature laboured the point of face-masks, there were two individuals in the waiting room maskless and not a word was said to them by either the masked receptionists or the masked nurses. Exemption by default rather than the asking of the question.

Anyway, I passed my test and it was all systems go until the morning of the 11th when I would test for COVID-19. Negative. Karen and Kevin arrived to drive me to my destination with fate. They had failed to have time to test themselves that morning but I was beyond caring and we all had masks on.

Hug-less goodbyes at the hospital entrance followed by the Mauritian porter taking me up to my room with a view. Was the Mauritius connection another positive portent? And, I did have a view. My room was Thameside and I looked across to The City and the comings and goings on the river. The early arrival, I had been dropped off by six-thirty, ended up being completely unnecessary. It was close to eleven before I was operated on. Interesting, for at the preassessment the ideal arrival time had been brought forward by thirty minutes. And I had complied, and then some.

The nurse had no interest in my home COVID-19 test result as she instructed me to take another. Negative.

I signed my life away, in duplicate if not triplicate. I can't recall seeing Mary-Jane before the procedure, but did see the anaesthetist, to whom I recited the whole life story ... well about when I was two-and-a-half and was having my first foot operation and how I had to be pulled out of succumbing to that first experience of anaesthesia. My mother could not repeat that enough, fair play. Like her allowing this child to still attend football matches after the Ibrox Park disaster. To this day I still cross my arms over my chest whenever in an unpleasant human crush, to allow ribcage movement should one tumble underfoot; don't worry what it would do to your matinée idol good lucks, especially as an Alsatian had destroyed them (that is the nose of the said looks) in the summer of 1966 ... do I digress?

Yes, my mother's repetition is now repeated by me, as it has been ever since I have had general anaesthetics outwith her physical presence whilst she was still alive and her memory since her temporal demise. Interestingly enough I cannot fully recall this conversation having taken place at the PRUH on 6th October, but it must have. Likewise the coming too on the 6th is vague, though I remember Karen holding my hand and wetting my lips with a tiny square of sponge on a stick before being returned to the ward.

One of the big pluses about going private, to my mind, had been the timeline. Register and be operated on; these unexpected hours of waiting could have been unnerving, perhaps they should have been. But all I could think about, *focus on* might be too strong, was the reversal of the stoma … no longer having this part of my body outside my body. How could I not damage it? As one of the stoma nurses had intimated when I expressed my concerns about falling on it. It was so pink and raw, when not covered in faeces …

Anyway, my only pre-op question as I was being taken to the theatre of operations was, should I empty my stoma bag first. How ridiculous, whilst also being very me. Twat, to the potential end.

As I disappeared into an anaesthesia induced mist, I came to in my room with The City view later that mid-June day. I was alive. My midriff was wrapped as though it belonged to an Egyptian mummy as I took a quick peek, no sign of the stoma … if still poking out it would be being extremely squashed under all this strapping.

I was alive.

Telephone calls to make … and in my memory I made them in the early afternoon, but that's the deception of the British summer for you. My WhatsApp calls to Karen, Tony and Paul took place at 18:19, 18:24 and 18:28; but not necessarily in that order.

I was alive.

Yes, this was the immediate post-op euphoria, still mightily doped no doubt, but currently pain free, care free. Free of the stoma. Man had it been a long eight months.

Some pain did kick in later than evening, but pain that paracetamol tablets could relieve. No morphine for this very soon-to-be sixty-eight-years-old.

But *happy birthday to me* was still a few days away.

For all my somewhat mixed views of Mary-Jane, she did visit me every day whilst I was in the

London Bridge hospital, week days at around 7AM as she then had the return journey to Orpington to make as she switched back into her NHS role and hope to find a parking space …

Post-op, other than general recovery, the main object was to have me poo. Mary-Jane would even telephone my mobile of an evening asking if I had been. Not quite in the tone of Hylda Baker's *Have you been Walter?* As ever it was a case of discharge as quick as possible and though I personally felt that what was issuing from my anus was hardly worth calling excrement I was discharged a day early. It would have actually been the morning of the 16th as opposed to the evening if the hospital had had their way but it was more convenient for both Karen and I to make it the evening. Karen and Kevin drove to the hospital then Kevin returned home by tube and train whilst Karen drove me home.

With regards to going to toilet however, the trouble had only just started.

I kept feeling I wanted to go, needed to go, but nothing. Yet I would be up countless times in the night to release the urge of the empty spasms for fear that if I did not, I would soil my bedding. And sleep took ages to come and it did so in short spells as the spasms were painful. It felt like a cramping of the sphincter, a build-up of the tension then a release of nothing, at most a dribble of soiling.

I could only imagine, as I eventually discovered, that there was not a generic recovering pattern to stoma reversals. Thank goodness for my aunts' former carer, as she was able to advise that there was no normal, some clients she had cared for took over a year to emerge from the operation trauma with consistent and continent bowel movements. A year! OMG, etc. Karen could see me involuntarily wince as the spasms built up. The body is an interesting piece of machinery as despite not visibly excreting, so to speak, my innards must somehow have been reducing my intake to a liquidised squirt as I didn't feel bloated or stuffed.

The false alarm straining was causing enough pain for me to be concerned at this and the virtually zero output, so I contacted the London Bridge nurse *responsible* for me and she contacted Mary-Jane. Once Mary-Jane had recovered from her annoyance (at my contacting a nurse before herself) she told me to turn up first thing the next morning, June 21st, at the Surgical Ambulatory Unit at the PRUH. There she examined my anus and advised that I had a sphincter tear, for which she prescribed some ointment and some anaesthetic needles, with which to inject my anus with in order to dull the pain. Right! Have you ever tried to inject your own anus. It would perhaps have been something I would have asked a lover to do but Karen, Tony? No. Tony had driven me to the PRUH that morning and was thankfully at his most *I will not accept no for an answer* at the PRUH's dispensary when they tried to fob him off with not having the Mary-Jane prescribed medication and could we go to King's at Denmark Hill. They found they did have it in stock. Thank you, Tony. Even that was not the easiest thing to apply, Mary-Jane making a loud and clear statement about how small an amount should be used. I used the end of a smallish wooden spoon to apply it, subsequent events resulting in it being applied for but the first week of the two recommended. (FYI, after much discussion with Karen I gave in and the spoon went into the refuse bag!)

Sue G arrived with lunch for all three of us that

Tuesday in the last full week of the month. Temperatures were rising in the drought summer of 2022 and so we agreed to sit and eat outside. My body-cringe spasms continued the visit to Mary-Jane regardless, even though it in itself had been reassuring in that there was nothing major wrong. As she said at one of our meetings *How often do you want to go?* True, but also not the point when you are having trouble *going* (i.e., shitting) in the first place.

Due to the unnerving sensation of feeling that I was always about to do a number two I now wore disposable men's nappies, day and night. Clean, twenty-four hours, upon twenty-four hours, as I would rush to the toilet as the unfilled urge picked up its intensity. Maddening.

Sue G witnessed my latest wince as we settled down to lunch, I nodded that I was okay. And as we had only just sat down, I released the natural tightening of my sphincter and did my first proper poo since the op ... since my stoma op ... since before the 4th October 2021. I sat there in my glory and finished my lunch.

It wasn't like that at all. Though relieved that I had been able *to go* I was uncomfortable sitting in my own mess ... a relief in itself. What sort of state would I have succumbed to if it was a pleasure wallow?

Sue G and Tony cleared up the remnants of lunch as I cleared off to the bathroom to tidy myself up. And poo further. Be careful what you wish for is often so apt. But I had been and that was another tick on the road to recovery, however stop-start it was and would continue to be and some.

*

I was surprised to learn on my London Bridge hospital discharge day that I would need to inject myself each evening so as to minimise the chance of post-operation blood clots. I sadly had one of the jobsworth nurses as my instructor, which did not work for either of us. He merely wanted to demonstrate whilst I wanted to practice ... half the liquid from that injection went elsewhere than intended, his physical rather than vocal intervention the cause. Well excuse me, it wasn't going to be my fault, was it ... private health customer and all.

Although I was initially quite brave doing it,

perhaps because of Karen's initial presence, I did however find it harder to do as day followed day. Perhaps this decline in aptitude was also due to the fact that I had started to slip down the potassium/C-diff slope. One evening I injected the liquid into the tendon of my upper thigh – which I had been advised to avoid. I realised why. Ouch! And a lingering *ouch* at that.

*

My mobility was still an issue, and I required a new set of carers, in this instance their line of duty was as sock and boot putters-on and takers-off morning and afternoon respectively. No set times, obviously. Thankfully none were observers. No, I did not miss Kim. The afternoon to evening visit being particularly irksome as it could well be as early as 4PM. How I sympathised with those who had no option but to be bedded at 4PM during midsummer as that's when the carer visited. In the mornings I could shuffle around in un-Velcro-upped boots until visited, usually by 10AM. Usually! Oh, to be able to bend sufficiently again to be able to put on my socks and boots by myself. So little to ask, yet it was virtually within a week of making this plea that it was to seem even more of a remote wish than ever.

To my credit, he types, I did try and assist the lives of these carers by advising them should I be absent prior to their undefined arrival, like when I went to have most of my stitches removed on the 27th June. Obviously, I went to have all my stitches taken out, Mary-Jane happened to leave at least four of mine in … which I removed over the next few weeks. Ed, back on his own road to recovery, did the needful sock and boot carer assist upon returning me home.

Thankfully the carer-controller knew of my likely plight from the reporting in of the morning carer of 30th June when I picked up her call the morning of the 1st.

Another month, another spell in hospital.

July 2022

The hospital dead hours, from a patient's point of view are 7 to 9 in the morning and 7 to 9 at night. The shift switch seems to take a total of four hours out of patient care each day. The beginning of each two-hour slot is perhaps mitigated in the morning with the arrival of breakfast; I would respectfully suggest that any evening mitigation is solely dependent on whether one has visitors occupying the first hour.

It took me no time to learn that the response time to my call button in the staff shift switch would be double that, if only, of during the other hours in the twenty-four. My problem was that my bowels could not adjust to when was convenient for the staff!

Since when were the staff allowed to choose which jobs they did or didn't do? I certainly found out those who cared from those who didn't do and those who did but carelessly.

When my scrotum was at its most engorged (full details to follow!), I could not reach to use the bottom wipes on myself. The number of times the cleaning of me was cursory, despite my pleas of *are you sure* being responded to with a curt *yes*; only for me to climb back into bed and find I was trailing khaki marks across my bedding. When said staff next had the pleasure of cleansing my behind, I would go and sit on my towel covered chair before returning to bed, at least then the towel could be put in the wash without me annoying the hard-pressed staff even more by asking for fresh bedding.

The best staff would actually anoint my anus with soothing creams once cleaned with disposable wet-wipes. The worst used the almost corrugated paper hand-towels to do a sandpaper clean. I do appreciate that the mess I created was extensive – but really? What d'you say? You literally have to take the rough with the smooth.

My next quibble is supper time. Well, it's not supper time at all, is it? Isn't it more teatime? Five o'clock in the afternoon! Do you realise how that makes time drag. DRAG! How it is psychologically damaging to those on the road to physical recovery to have this virtual ending of their day by 17:30 of an afternoon. I can only assume that this is to do with the catering staff's working day not the patients' welfare. Please don't say it's to benefit the ill, the unwell patients are not at the stage of caring about meal times.

And, who monitors whether the unwell or even well staff are eating their meals. All this process is so random, hit and miss. The catering staff will eventually remove a tray, especially if the patient in question cannot answer the *finished?* question. The reporting down to chance, the untouched or barely touched tray being spotted by a diligent member of staff. Care, within lies a multitude of sins.

Why do the hospital menus walk? What is their Ebay collector's item value? But they do walk.

The catering staff must have considered me somewhat doolally for asking day-after-day for a rundown of the meal choices. Well, without a menu to hand how was I to know whether a new palate teaser had been added to the à la carte menu …

Actually, being in possession of a menu can be dangerous to freshly sown stitches, such the rib-tickling mirth engendered by being advised to contact the ward hostess (how sexist!) for between meal snacks. Really! Ward hostess! Between meal snacks! Get back to your own planet mate. And take the menu with you. Still here and *Missed a meal?* Do not fear; *if you have missed a meal we offer a selection of hot and cold options. Please speak with your Ward Host(ess) or a Nurse outside of the regular meal service times.* Good luck with that. Consider yourself lucky to be in hospital and not out on the street where you'd likely end up with a slapping if not worse for your impudence. Can't you read the CLOSED sign. And as for spelling. Turia as turai as ridge gourd probably!

Snacks and Beverages: - *Your Ward Host(ess) will provide you with fresh water, hot and cold beverages and a selection of snacks throughout the day. Please ask a member of staff for any additional snacks or beverages.* A vodka martini, shaken not stirred?

Meal Ordering: - *Simply request any Breakfast options from your Ward Host(ess) during service time. They will then visit you to take your lunch and dinner meal orders.*

Please, you in the back row, control your mirth … is this belly laugh to see if one's stitches will hold?

Dietary Information and Coding: - *If you have been told to follow a specific diet, look for the dietary symbol on the menu next to the item. An explanation of the symbols used is provided below.* Time for the caveat … *It is for guidance only and should be used at your discretion.* I would respectfully, as well as disrespectfully (actually), suggest that when ill all this verbiage means diddly-squat, you have enough of a problem focussing on the speed with which your hostess rattles through the menu … as most patients aren't actually provided with one. On my two patient visiting trips since my own PRUH incarcerations neither patient had seen sight of a menu let alone knowing of their existence. Their troubleshooting visitor resolved this. And it was during these visits that I laughed out loud at the above. Ideals very, very far from being achieved. The specific diet choices do not cover low fibre and as I enquired of a hostess I was known to when visiting Ed (back in hospital having fractured his collar bones), how come the hostesses' computers don't advise of a patient's dietary requirements for, especially upon admission or immediately after a procedure the patient is in no state to know if he is choosing something *easy to swallow* or *high energy*. He's not about to head off to a gay disco buffet. Allegedly patient turnover, as in speed of discharge not number of deaths, means that this is not viable as the software could not keep a sufficiently accurate track of the inmates changing needs, *nil by mouth* changing to *clear liquids* for example. Yet, as I know from my own pneumonia experience the handwritten update erasing my *nil by mouth* was overlooked. There is no perfection, I do understand that. But at least if the hostesses' tablets were used there would be an audit trail.

The above bed board information, as previously moaned about may have the formal name of the patient but not necessarily their known-by name, the name of the consultant or surgeon or doctor they are under, the name of that shift's nurse in charge and finally their allowed intake if qualified. The nurse in charge's name is solely dependent on that nursing individual. Been there, seen that!

*

It many ways each incident seems like but an additional twist of the coil. How tight must it be wound before the inevitable SNAP! happens?

How in control was I? Would SNAP! be a choice or taken out of my actual control? Was the phlegmatic me a thin surface veneer?

Actually, a daily re-mix of emotions.

Like a review of what I had expected from my stoma reversal. I hadn't expected to be back in hospital less than a month after the *successful* operation, but I had also not anticipated recovery to be instant with a return to the summer of 2021.

As previously stated, Mary-Jane took most of my stitches out, forty minutes after my scheduled appointment, on Monday the 27th of June. I say most as, worth repeating, I removed four more in the weeks that followed. My fault, obviously! As I was talking (answering her questions) whilst she needed me to lie perfectly still.

If I had started to feel unwell then it was nothing compared to the deterioration that followed. I had a dental appointment on the Tuesday afternoon which Ed kindly ferried me to. Anne and Martin had volunteered to be there for me but head colds understandably meant they didn't want me to be infected. Ed resumed the duty he had performed the previous night as my chauffeur.

The Wednesday is something of a slow burning blur. Geoff, my builder friend, called to fix the locking mechanism, actually the unlocking mechanism, of the sunlounge door. I remember sitting watching him in silence, no doubt he moaned about his partner, but that day I offered up neither tea nor cake nor sympathy, such the state of my brain's decline. Fuck off Geoff! Heal yourself … for I was spiralling down in a bad way.

Onto Thursday morning, I woke to find that I had soiled my nappy so badly that the discharge had seeped onto the sheet. Though I managed to both wash and dry the fitted sheet there was no energy to make up my bed. Thank goodness, in more ways than one, for Kevin's arrival. Yes, Karen is my attendant carer but she was indisposed with her father's health issues and had kindly delegated Kevin to check-in on me. I was on the point of collapse.

In Kevin's presence I telephoned the doctor's surgery and was amazed that I was offered an appointment at 5PM that same afternoon. Kevin said he would stay to drive me there as there was no way I could walk it, plus I was still weeks away from when I could sensibly drive. The doctor phoned back within about thirty minutes of my initial call asking if I could come now.

Dr. Nava listened to my chest and took my blood pressure and advised me to go straight to A&E. He gave me a letter to hand in on arrival. I know I was feeling sleepier and sleepier. Kevin took me back home so that I could feed Gizzy and collect my toothbrush and mobile phone …

By now you will know my A&E aversion but today this ragdoll had no volition.

Kevin had to help me out of his car at A&E, and leave me there. Retrospectively, Karen tells how

Stoma in a teacup

he hated doing so as I was so wan and listless. But we are rule observing individuals, and whilst others may flaunt them …

Anyway, thank goodness the triage process was relatively swift for I was desperately trying to keep awake in case I missed hearing my name being called out. My intrinsic nosiness assisted, as this one bloke kept refusing to have his bloods taken whilst complaining about not being seen … and I kept thinking *does he or doesn't he want help*. I was seen, and wheeled out of his sight to be met in a behind doors A&E cubicle by a doctor and nurse. The number of times you are asked your name and date of birth is legend, and on occasion even the first line of one's address. All the while your name and DOB are attached to your wrist.

I have felt this ill before. Where in some ways you don't actually realise how ill you are. The plateau, or more accurately the basement has been reached, and there is a calmness almost a serene feeling. The modern day *whatever!*

I was also used to having a canula attached, what I did not become used to was how some nursing staff were naturals at this task whilst others showed their dread as they invariably felt pin-cushioning patients was acceptable. Where possible Surgical 9 devolved this task to two specific members of staff. Hard luck if you had to give blood samples or have a canula inserted whilst they were not on duty.

Whatever (see!) the body had decided there was something still working in my mind for I clocked the look of shock and concern from said doctor's and nurse's respective expression as something flashed on the beeping screen behind my head.

'What?' I asked.

'You must have a very strong heart,' the doctor was to inform me. 'With your potassium level your heart should have stopped.'

By and large a law abiding and obedient fellow I obviously had flaunting moments …

At this stage, lying there, potassium levels meant diddly-squat to me. The basement level was acceptably comfortable. The mind whilst not totally numb was not over concerned as I drifted. When able to vocalise a retentive enquiry, I was informed that my potassium level upon admission had been 2.3. This meant nothing to me, then as now really, but it seems that 3.6 to 5.2 millimoles per litre is the desired spread.

No-one, however, was able to advise how this set of circumstances had come to pass. The focus once I was being given a potassium infusion was on my diarrhoea. Oh joy! Something else to throw into the mix. C.diff! What, never heard of it? Ditto!

How I wish that had remained the case. Two weeks of hell were to follow. Putting the rest of the twelve months' spells in hospital into a rose-tinted perspective. Yes, I exaggerate … no hospital visit, let alone stay, is anything but a dire experience.

But this was the pits. Veritably the basement (obviously word of the month), even as my physical being tried its darndest to recover it was plagued with further issues. All of this whilst I was incarcerated in an isolation room within Surgical 9 ward.

It was never fully explained to me how I contracted *clostridioides difficile*, or where from, in the first place. From what I have read I have to assume it was as a result of the courses of antibiotics received from London Bridge hospital. But I had it, and one of its main symptoms ... diarrhoea. This said, didn't I have diarrhoea anyway, as part of the whole stoma reversal process?

And more bad news if you read up on C.diff ... it causes an infection in the large intestine ... the colon. Hadn't mine JUST been popped into my body, and stitched-up? Was it a right stitch-up? Death was also mentioned ... was I the non-cat with nine lives? If so, how many had I used up ... birth, drowning, anaesthesia ... all three before reaching that number in age. STOP IT!

Initially I really wasn't well enough to care, at some level. Yet, at another I was and the annoying nag that as a personality trait my mother used to find the most irritating was what the hospital staff also had to deal with. You know the type of kid, where you blithely say *later* hoping that they'll forget but they don't and just keep on reminding you *is it later yet*.

Yes, the first weekend was still very much a get better one. I didn't even really care what was going on at Wimbledon ... on the day before admission I had actually gone to bed before the end of the Andy Murray match, before the end of the second set. Right there you have how ill I was becoming.

My own private room in an NHS hospital, how lucky was I? NOT! I was in isolation, so said the blurb on the inside of my closed door. The said door must be closed at all times. The staff all wore COVID masks anyway, but aprons and gloves were also de rigueur except when they weren't. On occasion my cornflakes' deliverer would remove an un-gloved finger from being submerged in the milk upon placing the bowl on my table.

The extent of my quarantine was either not fully explained to me till the beginning of my first full week, or at least that's when I began to understand what was going on, for my WhatsApp messages advised potential visitors of the potential health risks to themselves. It did keep them away.

Not all. The mentally insane or gay still visited. Sorry … but we haven't had flippancy for a while …

Despair! What a mild sounding word for conveying how I actually felt. Dear Reader, the plus side, from your perspective, is that rock bottom has now been reached. Honest! Would I lie to you? Trust me, I don't, or try not to lie to myself, why would I to you? Though I managed, I think, to laugh at times with my stoic visitors, I think it was more gallows humour than genuine mirth.

You cannot really fall any lower than eating your evening meal, served at if not before 5PM, while simultaneously seated on a commode with diarrhoea flowing into the papier-mâché receptacle. Really? Really! Twice. That is on two occasions. Your meal is served whatever your state of readiness, whatever your state of indisposition. *In flagrante delicto!* The joy of isolation when you know that *can you come back in ten minutes* means no food.

Considering life since this particular release from hospital, one of the facts of this stay was that I did not once soil my bed. Yes, I spent ages on either the commode or the toilet itself. If the bedding was soiled at all it was as a result of poor arse-wiping not being caught short. This also explains away my lethargy and general air of tiredness, for I found sleep so hard to come by. Other than finding it so hard to be comfortable was the fear of the bowels opening without my being in position, so to speak. Spasms would go on all night, which I would work on controlling until I felt that there was sufficient force behind the dam for the sluice gates to be opened. (Nowadays it seems I sleep without spasms and discharge botty dribbles in my sleep.)

The C.diff induced diarrhoea did have a pattern, an infuriating one ... that both the staff and I found equally annoying even though for different reasons. Basically, and grossly, there were two initial large discharges, fairly close together, or close enough that you realized that you hadn't *done yet*; followed by a lengthy gap that made you think that that was it and you should press the call button. Once this was done you could almost guarantee that you would need to go right away, or better still as the staff member came in to clean you up. And I felt guilty, or was made to feel guilty. *Sorry, five more minutes.* It was awful. And I was sorry. Sorry but helpless.

At home, post my stoma reversal, where I both found it initially difficult to bend forward and didn't want to stretch anything unnecessarily by bending forward, I had bought off Amazon, a cheap plastic gadget that you wrapped your toilet tissue around and then used to wipe your bottom with minimal bend. Simple, eh?

As if having your bottom wiped was not potentially humiliating enough, I made a new discovery … the swelling to end all swellings!

I had taken to wearing diaper pads within my disposable hospital underpants in case of accidents. After this particular bottom clean, I was placing the pad back in situ for the nurse to pull my pants over when I discovered what I was tugging at was myself, not the nappy pad. Myself! I could not believe the size of my testicles.

It took all that second Saturday and into the evening before I was seen by a doctor. The nurses were concerned, one had mentioned the legs swelling even before I had become aware of what was going on between my legs.

It was as if my scrotum was a fully opened accordion. I could no longer close my legs comfortably; I was inflamed from the waist down. Majorly. Interesting not my actual penis, it had

Stoma in a teacup

blistered and shrunk into my scrotum as though the man in the moon was wishing to hide. I had to sit down to urinate or hold the papier-mâché vessel fully over the pin-prick penis; otherwise, mess ensued.

The doctor's visit was less than satisfactory, she told me there was nothing wrong with my scrotum, with an underlying *man-up, don't waste our time*. I wondered what sort of men she had slept with if she thought my vast expanse of scrotum was normal, my mind going on to consider what other options she may choose, but still, what lay between my legs was not normal and it was painful.

After the 8th of July the only doctors who came near me were no older than twelve. Obviously not, but so young. One at the weekend was so dressed for summer and as I had misplaced my woke switch I thought that he was an orderly. Slap wrist Neil. Right. But give me a break.

Talking of which and back to the swellings. I now had a constant pain in my right foot, and could no longer put any weight on it. No, I did not want morphine. Really! Paracetamol would have to do. But my head? They had absolutely no idea what this was doing to my state of mind. Was that the end of me ever being able to play tennis again, would I be able to walk unaided again, would I be able to walk … questions that were dispatched into a vacuum of my own creation. I no longer attempted to reach the toilet the commode had to brought to my bedside. Yes, the foot pain was that bad, it felt broken. Having previously thought quite highly of my pain threshold acceptance there was no way I was accepting this. Which I did realise was as much mental as physical, if not more so.

The good nurses did what they could and the junior doctors or registrars or the folk with stethoscopes eventually advised that it was all down to my albumin levels a side effect of the antibiotics I was being given to combat the C.diff, whilst seeming far less perturbed than me or the nursing staff. From the groin down the stickman that I was had become the Michelin-man. Sumo gross!

One duty nurse took such pity on me that she changed my mattress for an air one. I was very much relieved that she was not on Surgical 9 duty the following day or subsequently for I had to ask for a switch back to the old mattress. Her kindness backfired as my swollen bits and pieces got trapped within the air mattress quilting, adding rather than relieving the discomfort.

Blaming the swelling on my low albumin levels meant that I was now put on water tablets to tackle this imbalance, as well as being given a different antibiotic to combat the recalcitrant C.diff whilst at the same time being told to maintain my level of liquid intake.

It is actually hard to maintain one's level of liquid intake when one's call button is not answered, not only not answered but switched off. No matter how many times the handyman was called to fix the call button in the ensuite toilet nineteen times out of twenty it would cancel itself prior to be answered. I spent tens of minutes pulling the chord to *on*; impotently screaming for someone to come and wipe my bottom clean.

That's a lack of response that can perhaps, though part of me remained unconvinced, be put down to technical issues but when I could see my bedside call light was on as well as hear its beep at the nurses' station outside my door and yet it was still over forty-five minutes before anyone responded …

Once I telephoned Surgical 9 from my mobile to request a jug of water as I had been waiting so long for my call button to be answered. And another time I asked Tony to phone the ward to request that they answer my call button and provide me with a jug of water. On this occasion they answered my call button whilst I was advising Tony on what I wanted him to say.

Was it the room's location, right outside the ward's hub? The nights I would scream in sheer frustration *shut the fuck up* at the volume of noise they generated, fine, be happy in your work, but please remember these are ill people who are trying to sleep to aid recovery. It was like flying on a red-eye full of stag or hen party-goers, or a red-eye where your nerves focused on your unshaven keynote speech too few hours away.

Blimey, that takes me back … a life of work and good health …

Bottom line is that death would have arrived before assistance on most call button occasions, to the extent that the last couple of days of my incarceration I would open my cell door and call for assistance. That worked. How to defeat the

Stoma in a teacup

object.

As I state over and over, quite rightly I feel, other than just because it's my story, the good nursing staff were EXCELLENT, so let down by the inadequate who were crap. Trust me, I no more wanted my bottom wiped aggressively than they showed their displeasure in performing the task. Even the ward sister, or whatever the modern nomenclature is was flakey. And sorry, I don't buy in to the over worked, not with regard to every occasion there was for interfacing. I feel my physical body deteriorates during any length of hospital stay. I enquired about a visit from an in-house physio. Wait for it. The sister advised me that the physio had visited whilst I was squatting in my ensuite, so obviously I was mobile enough and didn't need any physio. Obviously! Stupid me. I didn't see the physio ...

Damaging to me both mentally and physically. During the course of a hospital stay I can almost see the degradation in the dexterity of my fingers through lack of use, be it in trying to open a yoghurt pot or retrieve a pill that has escaped across my tray-table. Without wishing to over dramatise I do not regain one hundred percent of my pre-admission flexibility after discharge, the degree in absolute proportion to the length of stay. Depressing, as my state of independence is so dependent on the flexibility of my digits.

This reminds me of my volition to walk unaided back in October of last year. I was initially surprised at how difficult, once up out of the bed it was to stand upright, let alone walk unaided. Yes, I had a marvellous array of metal staples by way of stitches up the middle of my torso, but still. I was an old man bent over a Zimmer frame. Was this really me? With word out that hospital release was not solely dependent on how I coped with my stoma I now had another goal in sight. A physiotherapist would turn up with various walking aids each day, as I became both more confident and more determined the equipment slimmed down. *See you tomorrow*, said Mario after Thursday's session, leaving me with a walking stick of a crutch that had a four-pronged base. I was like a teen with their first set of wheels, almost. Except Mario was a no-show on Friday. Do that to Neil at your peril. Right, I thought. I was already able crutch assisted to ambulate to the toilet, but during the course of Friday night, though I carried the crutch I stopped using it. I was independently mobile. And by the Sunday I no longer carried the crutch. Oh, and I thanked Mario on the Monday of my release for having spurred me on.

A downside of my cussed determination was that the ubiquitous Cindy complained to Roger in the bed to my left about his laziness compared to mine. Roger also had a stoma but always pressed his call button for it to be emptied or changed. *Nothing wrong with fingers*, I heard Cindy admonish him whilst wishing myself invisible within my bedclothes. Roger was a quite unwell cancer patient and I felt bad that my behaviour reflected badly on him. Other than the fact that Cindy should not have been comparing, considering her views of my knife and fork holding and inability to believe I could tell my right boot from my left, did she actually have any appreciation for what Roger was going through?

Whilst having a moan … I don't know if it was down to me being blessed with a body that tends not to exude BO five minutes after a shower, but gone it seems are the daily wash either given or offered to the patient. When I was well enough to give myself a modest wash it was generally at my instigation not the staff's. And as for when I was too ill, when a wash would have been refreshing as well as diversionary, they tended not to be forthcoming. Was it to do with how messy my posterior was post-reversal? But that doesn't explain the lack of washing proffered during stoma bag stays; though, on all visits, once mobile and strong enough, I was happy to shower in privacy, and play Russian roulette with the floor surface. Now how is this for ridiculous … you have a non-slip shower floor, great, but as soon as a wet foot steps off of it you are on a veritable ice-rink. I used to have to step on to a towel (there are no bathmats) to dry my feet before advancing. Crazy! Funny how there's no health and safety where it is actually needed. Towels? There are no bath towels, they are all hand towel size … one could go insane.

Then … yes, there's more. The daily bed making isn't at all daily, nor is sheet changing. I do appreciate staff shortages, honest, but. Actually, no buts. It is an utter disgrace, especially considering how hard I worked during my C.diff stay not to soil the bedding and yet the hurried and careless botty wiping resulted in a series of *skid marks*.

My favourite, not, incident with said *sister*, arose over my bringing to her attention, in a Neil-Andrews-altruistic manner, the corner cutting of the nightshift nurse-in-charge. I had two points to make, which I didn't feel were pedantic, as their behaviour was distinct from that of their colleagues I wanted to ascertain whether the fact that they only did one lot of obs a shift was acceptable and secondly that they did not make up obs for the two lots they missed out. Observations are blood pressure, blood oxygen level and temperature; other nightshift staff observed at the start, the middle and end of their shift. My obs was that on consecutive nights said individual did but a solitary observation.

Long-winded as this is I honestly thought I was being helpful. So, what does Sister Morphine do, she just goes and tells the nurse in question about *my complaint*, it was a fucking obs, and it didn't belong to me. It belonged to her as management. So not only does she not couch it in a general you know obs should be taken three times a night but also, by the way, it was the patient in room 273 who reported you. She relays this to me as she is about to go off duty with the said nurse back on the nightshift. I sent WhatsApp messages to Karen and Tony and Paul that night … just in case a pillow got trapped over my face in the night. That'll put paid to any future whistleblowing he may have up his surgical gown … thank you and have a good evening, Sister Morphine!

I survived the night. It transpires that obs are taken for fun, three times a nightshift is totally unnecessary unless you are dying, and I wasn't by this stage, and the nurse in question didn't like to wake patients unnecessarily. Don't make me laugh. Trying to allow us to sleep seemed the unnecessary part of a hospital stay. Did the sister make it up as she went along. What was the point?

The actual point was that it was not worth thinking about. I was a sixty-eight years old patient not an unnecessary NHS time-and-motion power point presenter.

Oh yes, how the NHS could do with funds … but isn't running out of pillow cases and baked potatoes more to do with bad management than lack of funding. The two issues need tackling together, not separately …

On my second Sunday I felt my stool was starting to solidify, in comparative terms. Obviously, the time had come to change the antibiotics I was on, so that within thirty-six hours the diarrhoea was back. Result, I heard whispered stage left.

Despair at believing that these twelve-year olds dressed up (at times) like doctors not only didn't care but didn't know what they were doing. Do your Mum and Dad know you're out? I had not seen a consultant since Friday the 8th. I think that was the last time I saw Mary-Jane on this visit. Her passing comment was one of too much cheese in my meals.

Okay Mary-Jane, now you have me onto hospital meals. The highlight of my days, the light of days in hospital was meal times. Well lunchtime for the 5PM serving of supper was somewhat bitter sweet, signifying the premature end of the day of another hospital day, the death bringer declaring the commencement of another long hospital night.

Unlike many, I actually found the food tasty if not exactly haute cuisine. But …

And there are a number of the word *but* to cover. First and foremost, sweetcorn. Why oh! why when we all understand that sweetcorn goes through any body, yes anybody's body, is it so plentiful amidst the menu. Even a chicken sandwich turns out to be chicken and sweetcorn. A cheese or ham sandwich turns out to be a handmade sandwich (gloriously advertised in the elaborate packaging) of two pieces of dry bread with a square of cheese or ham in between. Am I repeating myself? Probably.

I had on this current stay been admitted with a critically low level of potassium and either simultaneously or soon after C.diff. Not once did a member of staff advise me to consume either orange juice or bananas for the potassium or avoid fibre for the C.diff diarrhoea. The fear with reference to the latter was whether I had lost my appetite or not. No fear! I had a voracious appetite, to the extent where I wondered whether I had worms. (Actually, a recurring nightmare of a theme, remind me to elaborate if I have the time and you the inclination to read about it.) I was actively encouraged to eat, despite the jet-propelled emissions. And I did. Though it was I who chose to be *sensible* like giving away my three-pack of digestive biscuits to Karen's Kevin.

Sensible? Mary-Jane obviously considered a lasagne or macaroni and cheese as not sensible. But dairy was highly recommended, although I knew that lactose was likely to encourage the trots as opposed to putting a halt to them. But then the dietician ... oh goodness me, YES, a dietician ... actually three times within four days. Laugh, please do. I still do. She was excellent and the second visit was at my request as her first had been interrupted by one of the twelve-year-old doctors, so I had not been able to fully concentrate on her words of wisdom.

A dietician. Amazing. I did enquire as to whether she also dealt with stoma patients, but was advised that they had their own dedicated dieticians. Perhaps she meant desiccated and I misheard as the twelve-year-old invaded my ear space. Perhaps!

Amazing though what can be provided if there is the will to push for a patient's welfare. And this is meant neither as in tongue-in-cheek mode nor in flippant throwaway mode but what she arranged for my top-up breakfast was a toasted bacon sandwich, sort of. Please, remember this is an NHS hospital, so two slices of toast, two individual pats of butter and two rashers of bacon delivered to my room in one of those take-away polystyrene containers. How neat is that? And very tasty too. So, the NHS monolith can be moved. Give the staff volition and patients who can interact appreciatively.

So politically incorrect, where's the hospital's woke police, for one of my favourite items on the menu was Scouse (beef stew) - a hearty one pot stew with diced beef, diced potato, carrot and swede. Yummy, yum! The dietician thought the pork and leek sausages was another dish I could tackle ... but it was served with mixed vegetables, which invariably included peas and the ubiquitous sweetcorn. Instructing me to leave the sweetcorn, peas, carrots, broccoli etc. when one is starving and there is no mix and match, no flexibility. Scouse (beef stew) is served with underlying hubcaps!

One of my other beefs is the obvious discrimination, whichever way you look at it – there is a *Cultural* heading that actually only consists of items that are solely South Asian, as they would appear on your local Indian restaurant's menu, though more than likely properly spelt. Or is the pedant harping on for harping on sake – turia or turai a ridge gourd regardless of spelling? Just saying. So, back to discrimination, should *Scouse (Beef Stew)* not appear under Cultural? And, why no West Indian no West African no East European items under the Cultural banner? Okay, I guess post-Brexit we can forget East European options! And, oh yes, there is another but, for there are already three types of curry listed amongst the main meals. And, as I'm on a roll, five out of a total of seventeen main meals dedicated to our ill Italians …yet try and find an Italian restaurant in Petts Wood these days … I side track you as well as myself.

Happy OTT woke day! You would really find it hard to make this all up. It's like one of my former flatmate Simon's favourite Tom Sharpe novels.

Tell me, as all meals are now ordered via the use of a digital tablet could not each patient's diet requirements be linked so that one is not allowed to order fibre or difficult to chew or non-vegetarian? Think how easy it would make everyone's life … the demented would not be harassed into making decisions that aren't actually decisions and might therefore be given a variety of foodstuffs; the diabetic would not be allowed to stray. Is the menu choice information put to any use other than the ordering of the inmates' meals? Would it be too difficult to have a linking feed where there was two-way communication.

A by-product could be a lack of waste. Currently, if I ordered a roast chicken dinner and wished to follow my low fibre diet, I would have to leave the stuffing and mixed veg, consuming only the chicken and potatoes. This applies to so much of the sweetcorn (and pea) infested meals …

More hot lemon sponge and custard please …

I realise there is no point mentioning, as I am about to, the 5PM supper delivery. For sure staffing in the sense of catering staff as well as nursing staff shift schedules no doubt make it sensible to have the evening meal partaken at that time and I am sure the more senior inmates like an early supper.

For myself, though I anticipated the meal it made the rest of the day drag on so … especially during the long daylight of early July, doubly especially if one is no longer actually dying. Sorry! I have reached the no shame stage. Okay, again.

Dear fellow patients, if able, please do say *hello* and *thank you* to the catering staff. Manners go a long way wherever you are. Honest, even if not initially it's like Chinese water torture, eventually you wear them down. Okay not all, on a visit Ed was witness to one who just plonked my tray down without giving me a chance to clear the table. My *thank you* was sarcastically tongue-in-cheek, but it was still stated.

As for my eventual July 16th release, was *Miss* Jones the catalyst or was it the cataclysmic weather forecast for the following week? Whatever! I had given up trying to understand how the sister's mind worked. On the Thursday Peter-the-train showed up with a bag of four croissants. As previously stated, Chinese water torture works wherever, whatever the discharge my appetite remained ferocious. Despite his cross between Clement Freud and Steptoe Père's disposition it was both good to see him and for him to visit. One of the things I actually liked about Peter-the-train was that he caught you off guard by his kindness that belied his favourite grumpy-old-git posturing. I polished off all four croissants before my 5PM supper. Pig out! I know, but they tasted so delicious, different, fresh, buttery … thank you.

And, bless him, he returned the next day, accompanied by another bag of four croissants as well as Chris Jones, aka *Miss* Jones. One of

Chris's main assets is that as the unabashed centre of attention no-one else need partake, his is a one-person show. They are an excellent visitor (I hope you have noticed the gratuitous woke pronoun that I have thrown in) for a patient who needs only nod, smile and laugh in the right places. And as for bolshy … well it's *Miss* Jones's way or no way. As he departed, he advised the sister, in his inimical full vocal discharge from my room's door, that I should be released as there was nothing wrong with me. I hadn't shown him my reduced but still somewhat swollen scrotum. There was no need, my legs were evidence of the swelling that I claimed travelled north. Did Chris's shouted into the ether comment have the sister take note.

Everyone was commenting on the impending record breaking temperatures, where for at least two days 40+ degrees was anticipated, was that a reason to chuck me out of my prison-like hospital room; even though I still had C.diff and was as infectious. Allegedly! That Friday, I only managed two of the croissants that Peter-the-train brought in, giving the other two to Sue H who popped in to see me that evening. Interesting that despite my contagion no-one snatched the croissants from her hand … surely, she was at risk? In fact, my guests would turn up in various states of PPE dress or undress. Mask, gloves and apron were de rigueur but also optional, ask the catering staff not the nurses. You have to laugh, and Sue H was going to have the croissants for breakfast.

*

Not a good luck charm as such, nor a talisman, more a marker, an aim – something to focus on. Somehow filthy glasses and a hospital stay went hand in hand, even in isolation. Go figure! So, I asked Karen if she could retrieve a handful of my spectacle wipes. Which she did. I decided that I would be discharged before using them all up. What makes us set these crazy illogical targets? Aren't the dangers of abject failure greater than any psychological gain? Is the benefit purely illusory? Yes and no. The delivery of the wipes was made whilst I was still unwell, and I made the conscious choice of not using one each day in case I ran out whilst still incarcerated. The rules of the game were mine and I was going to win. There was nothing in the rules that said I had to use at least one wipe a day. Kidology? It's whatever sees you through. The innermost make-believe world of the single soul.

I don't know how they managed to become so grubby. Yes, I was probably wearing them as much as if I'd been up and about, but there was no extra lens touching, and my room was cleaned at least every second day if not every day. One of life's many mysteries. Okay, no need for facetiousness.

The outcome, my games worked, I won; I was discharged with wipes to spare. I could see clearly now …

*

Yes, for whatever reason I was suddenly to be discharged. Enough of me was enough of me, C.diff infected regardless. The morning of my discharge there was a hiccough, well there had to be. As I had C.diff it was decided not to transfer me back home in an ambulance that was returning home four other individuals. Makes sense, no way would I want to pass C.diff on. An hour or so later I am transported home, no, not on my own, but with a bed ridden elderly lady who needs dropping off at Orpington hospital. She obviously didn't need to be isolated from me. Age? Lack of care? Indifference? What?

EXPLAIN YOURSELVES?

But I was home. Phew! And phew! again, even if Tony and Sue G met me at my own front door looking like a couple from the X-files awaiting the invasion of the alien Neil. Phew! Followed, mostly, by a whoosh! Be grateful. Be thankful.

I was a month on from the stoma reversal surgery and was therefore a bit more bendy around my middle but the tree trunk legs remained. I could put my boots on but not do them up nor could I think of getting socks on the job my carers were doing for me morning and evening prior to this latest period of hospitalisation. However, I couldn't have care visitors now, could I? It was like having COVID-19, I was in self-isolation, no passing of C.diff to the general public. From a safe distance Tony and Sue G organised and had lunch with me before beating a hasty retreat. It turns out that their nurse daughter-in-law to-be had put the willies up them with regards to C.diff, and, understandably, Sue G was concerned with regards to her nonagenarian parents. Bye then.

To keep me on my toes the hospital telephoned to advise that I had been discharged with a shortfall in my medication. Great! Just, great. Unfortunately, the person (sounding of the she gender) at the other end of the phone could not inform me which of the antibiotics the missing were from. She then told me to come to the hospital pharmacy to collect the medication. I politely, but with a trace of tearful frustration in my voice, explained that apart from not being in a position to drive I was also in isolation because of C.diff. *Oh right, I shall have them couriered over.* Right? Wrong in fact, for the missing tablets never showed up and on the Monday my doctor's surgery told me not to worry about it. And the cliché follows, easier said than done.

Thank goodness Karen was coming to stay, she would tide me over this unease. She also took photos of my legs on the Monday and the Friday, so that we could send to the doctor to show the lack of progress in a return to an albumin equilibrium. If diarrhoea was an indication of C.diff then I was still infected ... LARGE. You can't wish away something so in your face, or in my case exuding from your bum.

The doctor said I could send off a sample on the Monday, which I duly did. Ed very kindly taking the sealed plastic bag round to the surgery for me. Job done but with little hope of a positive outcome. Something in my tone must have sent surgery alarm bells ringing, or my thigh photos, for I was to receive a home visit from my doctor. It was something of a surreal experience. He intimated, without stating as much, that he had expected to find me living in squalor … and I had done no special pre-visit tidy-up, plus the lady-who-does hadn't since June the 30th. He told me to give my legs time and would I like some happy pills until the legs' swelling reduced. No, it's the lack of physical improvement, with no timeframe indication, that is bringing me down, not being down because of my physical condition. There is a huge difference. Happy pills indeed, enough to make me depressed.

*

Dear Chief Executive,

MENU

Whilst I appreciate, if there is to be a reply, it will be handed to a member of your management team to compose I wanted the matters I raise below to be from a sight point of view recorded as addressed to you.

Why are menus so elusive? This is a fact not solely experienced from my own hospital visits of 2021 and 2022 but from visiting friends in the last couple of months. Neither even knew of the menu's existence. On both occasions I had to pester the duty staff nurse to find one. FIND ONE! I advised my friends to hang on to them, like gold dust. Do patients actually take them home? I appreciate that over time some would break down through wear and tear but I would respectfully suggest that as with a bed, gown, slipper-socks etc. upon ward admittance that a menu is as essential as a jug of water – whether NIL BY MOUTH or not is written on the board behind the patient's head.

Your patients undoubtedly have different mental capabilities and capacities during their hospital

Stoma in a teacup

stay, but if a menu was available on each tray-table then at least their nearest or dearest could assist, failing that the ward staff whose care the patient is in, failing that the ward host(ess).

Ward host(ess)! Do you, yourself, actually believe in the term and all it implies? In my experience the ward host(ess) expects the patient to have knowledge of the menu, but with a sigh can start to recite the options at machine gun speed if pressed. A vacant stare of a response meaning the meal choice is handed to the ward host(ess) to make. In my humble opinion, apart from dismal quartermaster management, this is why the PRUH has, during my stays, run out of the likes of baked potatoes. Really? Yes, really – on more than one stay. The first thing recited off of the menu, the only thing remembered.

Now tell me, sweetcorn – one of

the most undigestible foodstuffs, how come it features so heavily in your menu. Even the halal chicken sandwich has sweetcorn. What's that all about?

With technology as advanced as it now is why can't patients' dietary needs be factored into the ward host(ess) tablets? We all wear hospital wrist bands with our hospital number appended. The scrawl behind the patient's head is at times undecipherable, at times out of date. I would respectfully suggest that say post-op the patient is in no position to know what diet, if any, they should be on, can the tablet not advise the ward host(ess)? Thus, assisting the latter in the job whilst also reducing the strain on the recovering patient. Take for example my own dietary needs; when I was recovering from my ileostomy and told by the stoma nurses that I should stick to a low fibre diet there is no such diet available on the menu. They then

Stoma in a teacup

advised that I order the likes of the roast chicken dinner but leave the mixed vegetables to the side, as well as the roasted shell of the roast potatoes and the sage and onion stuffing ball!

Whilst I appreciate that you all have to comply with the current world of woke, there are four *cultural* menu items on the Spring & Summer menu, all targeted to South Asian culture, fine, but listed in main meals are another three curries. I could be flippant and mention the five meals deriving from Italian cuisine ... and should the beef stew really be annotated as Scouse?

I must admit that it was not until I was actually discharged, and became a hospital visitor, that I read the small print, in a turn of phrase sense, on the menu. I wasn't aware that snacks and missed meals could be ordered *throughout the day.* I would dare

343

say that the verbiage on the menu was written with more staff in mind than the PRUH actually has. The ward host(ess) is seen once or twice a day at best. The person who plonks your meal down cannot be described as a ward host(ess); a visitor of mine was witness to the mute delivery of my supper with no patience given to clear my tray-table. These employees are also those that tend during the day to deal with the replenishing of the fresh water jug, though again, in my own experience, this is more often than not done by the nursing staff, if done at all. Twice during my stay of July 2022 either myself or a friend phoned, yes, in my case from my bed in an isolation room, the ward to ask if my water jug could be replenished as my call button remained unanswered for over forty-five minutes. (If I had had the presence of mind, I would have taken the phone to the toilet too as the call button was regularly unanswered for an unacceptable length of time, even when not out of order. The latter was reported but attempts to fix it were not successful.)

Have a nice day.

*

Whilst the Chief Executive is cogitating over my letter … WORMS!

Back in the day, my mother was convinced I must have worms. Convinced! All I did, allegedly was eat, but remained as ever as emaciated as any self-respecting Biafran child, but without the engorged belly, whilst my rosy-cheeked, and a-tad plumper brothers were the picture of health. Great Aunt Jean, a very soon-to-be retired district nurse thought it would be worth treating me for worms. *Let's be doing the lot of ye.* She announced on one of her passing-through visits as she withdrew a bottle of Antepar syrup from her well-worn leather dispensing bag.

The upshot was that the worms were passing through my brothers and not me. My mother merely shrugged at the perplexity that my condition continued to generate.

*

Oh, Nels Nels Nels! The need for diversion. Light relief. Thank you, Karen.

It can be the smallest, littlest, tiniest, quirkiest, okay I am sure you are with me by now, thing that can make a difference to a day. Everyone, including Karen, is used to my almost American style *candy* dish, its contents on this C.diff rescue stay where those round Lindt chocolate truffles. Karen's discovery one hot July afternoon, as I had a siesta, was that whilst the usually quite firm outer shell was somewhat softer to the bite the day's heat had literally liquidised the centre to an almost different confection. Definitely a different eating sensation. Divinely delicious. Even! We laughed and joked about how to market it and what Kevin would make of it when Karen tried them out on him.

Subsequently, I must confess to being somewhat partial to eating Lindt truffle balls in this liquified state, to such an extent that I have been known to place a couple in the sunlounge so as to alter their sold-as consistency.

Stoma in a teacup

*

Having often wondered why someone as busy as me found hospital stay's so boring I was consoled on a recent visit to a friend who like me has packed days when at home stated the same. Jean is in her late eighties has Parkinson's and of late has found herself in hospital a fair bit through fractures from falls. Obviously, I don't know how her brain works for her to come to the same conclusion as me, I just know that I cannot function as me anywhere near a hundred percent within the hospital environment. There is a stultifying numbness that seeps into me like Scotch mist, it eats away at pro-activity. The placid zombie lies prostrate ... waiting for the next interruption. Interruption if in a four-bed side ward; the call button to be answered if in an isolated room. I accept that staff shortages exacerbate this comatose state, in that if there aren't enough physios around to give one the time and input then there aren't. I don't have the answer to stimulation other than occupational therapy. The trouble is that the patients do not fit an identikit. On all my visits the shapes and sizes have been as varied as from a child's Mr Potato Face kit, and I would dare to venture that the majority of modern-day hospital staff are less able to give patients the oomph they would have received forty or perhaps even as recently as thirty years ago. Cultural differences? Again, not woke, but sod it. Some facts can't be woke. And I am gay, disabled and a Scot born in Mauritius. With a huge flippancy quotient. Joking (or flippancy) aside there is also training and expectation.

This is about me. I accept that some are happy to just idle their days away with vacant stares. Some have no option as vacant stares are now their state. But other than the second half of my four-day *dehydration* stay, where I suddenly snapped out of the anaesthetic fug and found a get up and go energy all other hospital stays induced lethargy. Even when I had my Thameside view from my private room at the London Bridge Hospital, the monotony of trying to remember the names of all the TFL river boots as they ferried their passengers in and out from the London Bridge City stop bore into my skull as the futile exercise it was. So mind numbing, that it verged on ruining the optimism that was coursing through my body at being shot of the stoma. At least here there was a TV screen, giving me the option of watching the tennis from

Queens. At the PRUH I would love to know the kick-back story for the useless media facilities attached above each bed. At least nowadays there seems no pretence at their usefulness. Ten years ago, when Auntie Betty went in to die there was still some semblance of said pretence that they were a great addition to the hospital facilities offered to the patient. I have yet to see one work.

My own fault or taste, but I have never been a great one with headphones and thus have not bothered with taking in the likes of a laptop or a tablet.

August 2022

So, once again the question of keeping a food diary is raised and I oblige. Apologies to you, dear reader, but someone has to read this stuff considering the diligence that went into maintaining a food diary for a second expanse of time, and for what? Exactly as pointless as the first time. Here's my GP wanting to feed me anti-depressants then being one of those in the profession asking me to keep a food diary. Knowing it won't be read, now that's depressing.

I decided that this particular diary should not only be input specific but also be as descriptive of my output. You lucky readers, here's three days of the ins and outs from August!

August 5th 2022

Input – a glass of water.

Output – 03:14 resistance futile, eventually! 06:24, explosive wind.

Input – two glasses of water, the daily medication, strawberry flavour Fortisip, bowl of cornflakes, banana, two mugs of tea.

Output – 09:37, clear liquid!

Input – Lucozade raspberry, two toasted bagels with sheep cheese, mug of miso soup, apricot and peach corner yoghurt, glass of apple and elderflower juice.

Output – 11:56, remains wet clear wind. Then at 13:03 major evacuation, would like to imagine a tad more solid than the current norm.

Input – cup of tea and five biscuits, half a glass of apple and elderflower juice, strawberry Fortisip.

Output – 18:17, nothing much.

Input – cod fillet in milk, with mashed potato, two glasses of red wine, Kefir yoghurt and raspberry jelly.
Output – 19:30 full flush out.

Input – eight chocolates.
Output – 20:38 … wind.

Input – four more chocolates, glass of water.
Output – 22:11 dribble; 23:44 wind and debris.

August 15th 2022
Output - 05:57, white bile … after two further in-bed discharges. Sleep apnoea returns like last night too!
WEIGHT - 67.5, so albumin levels continuing to flatten out.

Input - the daily medication, banana flavour Fortisip, bowl of cornflakes, banana, two mugs of tea, two glasses of water.

Output – 08:41 a worthy dump.

Input – mug of sweetened coffee, two chocolate chip cookies. Mashed potato with goats' cheese, a glass of apple and elderflower juice.
Output – 13:14, more pesky clear bile.

Input – ice cream and strawberry jelly.
Output – 14:17, that felt like a pretty reasonable and somewhat solid discharge.

Input - banana flavour Fortisip.
Output – 17:47 but a dirty dribble. 19:12 and more of the same.

Input – a glass of water, chicken pakora, one large glass of red wine, paneer tikka, pilau rice, roti, a glass of water, a glass of red wine.
Output – 21:51 more clear liquid with impressive wind.

August 25th 2022

Output – 02:03 very dirty and extensive runny discharge. 06:01 dirty drizzle.

Input – strawberry flavoured Fortisip, glass and a half of orange juice, two mugs of tea, mashed banana between two slices of white toast. Belgian chocolate choux bun, mug of coffee.
Output – 11:39 worthy discharge and no wind. 12:12 more? Yes.

Input – breaded ham sandwich on white with mustard, rice pudding with strawberry yoghurt, glass of water.
Output – 13:17 same old.

Input – chocolate cake, mug of coffee.
Output – 16:17 same.

Input – pitta bread and tapenade, red wine.
Output – 19:15 same.

> Input – more red wine, beef casserole, mashed potato, broccoli and cauliflower florets, apple crumble and custard.
> Output – 22:37 mostly wind, a lot of it dry.

But I was stoma free and the discomfort originating from July's hospital stay was dissipating and my head was in a much better place. I was dealing with the incontinence of my bottom pretty well, I felt, both mentally and physically. A somewhat false dawn as the premise was that this would be a relatively short-lived indisposition of a condition. And I dutifully did the sphincter clenching exercises, as advised by my GP as well as Mary-Jane, even though I wondered *why* for I was in total control of my bowels during my waking hours. So, if I had control when out and about and not near a convenience why did I lapse at night? There was no obvious answer. Not one with a solution, medical or otherwise. It did start to haunt me a tad as it recalled the nightmare of my urine bed wetting that went on and on beyond even my mother's tolerance. If that wasn't a forehead stamp of disability then what was it? I can't recall being seen by any medical practitioner about that and did it stop as I switched to discharging semen as opposed to urine? Go figure!

There was also another fear, all too real, that in no time I would have another blockage, followed by the removal of a further thirty centimetres of ilea and the ultimate joy of a stoma needing a bag … here I go again!

Prior to my admission to hospital in January 2020, with the blockage that had made me finally switch my doctor surgery, I had for most of my adult life had my stomach cramps treated as IBS. Cramps that I recalled starting from my early teenage years in Scotland. Yet, all along it was AMC.

Even when following my low fibre diet during the stoma days I had had wind aplenty, and though I was basically still sticking to a low fibre diet post-reversal I was still plagued by wind, the majority wet, so there was no freedom to fart, as it would mean messing my clothing. The nightly incontinence issues were basically wet winds escaping from between my buttock cheeks, on the whole waking me up, but not always, especially if only a dribble, for tending to sleep on my side not all created damp patches of enough substance to produce the wake-up trigger. Fascinating stuff? It's called part of the recuperation process. Remember I was housebound, no driving and was not supposed to do any lifting … a full watering can was definitely out of bounds. The drought was in full swing with a date set for the hosepipe ban. But I was realistic about the garden and it was what it was, I was not going to fight it. Now that I could envision a next year, that potential in itself was enough to let the drought do its worst. The havoc would be sorted in 2023. I had a specific target left to achieve in 2022, my holiday to witness the bat migration originally booked for November 2020.

September 2022

By the time I had finished it, *Absolution in Neutral* was my first completed novel for twenty years. I had dabbled at short stories and travel tales in the intervening years but not applied myself in any shape or form to a novel. Lack of discipline or the fear of not having the required discipline to apply myself amongst the reasons. Another was the enormity of the chasm all the blank pages present when you have all the time in the world. And when I eventually restarted *Absolution in Neutral* on January 1st 2021, I had all the time in the world. Another COVID 19 lockdown was in force and I was going nowhere at full speed. Yet, it was not until the end of the first month's writing that I announced what I was up to. For myself I needed that first month of writing at least five hundred words every day for the New Year's resolution to manifest itself sufficiently for me to believe *yes, I can do this*.

The point is?

Writing with AMC fingers I had not been aware of the actually less than subtle changes to my adapted style of typing.

My first novels were all handwritten and re-written, scored out, added to; then typed up. I actually typed up all bar my first (and discarded novel, dear *Tacker Tomes*), kindly typed up by Bunny, back in the day … but he had such a job reading my writing that it seemed simpler if I took on the typing myself, once self-satisfied with the manuscript.

So novel writing progressed through the Eighties as well as into the Nineties along the same lines, except from *True Falsetto* onwards I had a PC and so the finished novels were typed into Word. Oh yes, all through this, I remained unpublished. Rejection letters with the accompanying MS thudding onto the doormat became a somewhat masochistic hobby.

I had started *Absolution in Neutral* back in the Nineties; allegedly as the final part of the Kevin Jones trilogy; it ended up as something else, sorry Kevin Jones! To a certain regard *Twelve o'Clock Feet* was written under similar circumstances to *Absolution in Neutral*, I was out of love and going nowhere and needed a purpose. Something to make me leave my bed? A vehicle to channel my depression through. A vehicle for my anger? A nasty little self-pitying novel of a frustrated disabled homosexual. Who could that be?

Thanks to Karen's encouragement that I should let it all out, I did. So that novel was completed. During that early summer of personal discontent, I actually had an editor, let's call him Roderick Brown. Roderick was very helpful, and the content of the novel grew and was instilled with a certain light to balance the depth of its inner darkness, until that is the misplaced jealousy of Roderick's partner meant he was no longer allowed to communicate with me. Allowed? Yes, I know, sounds abusive to me too …

Stoma in a teacup

And back to the point ... the point. I used to type using the tips of two fingers, one on each hand, almost touch typing of sorts as I typed so much that I could be a slow yet reasonably accurate touch typist. Modesty. One of my bosses used to joke with his boss about my typing speed; he would not risk doing so now with the woke police, that is if he was still alive. Bless you Chuck. However, before his demise he did foresee that secretaries could be dispensed with, or at the very least have their titles changed to administrative assistants, with a shift in gender balance along the way, as having PCs and Word allowed one to complete many of the previously handwritten, and thus handed down, tasks. Take a letter self!

As stated, or will be stated elsewhere, between *Twelve o'Clock Feet* and *Absolution in Neutral* I complied three collections of shorts. And I have no recall of how I typed them up, as in finger use. I would put this down to the fact that the writing of all three was not as concentrated as the writing of a novel. Compilations tend to be less of a concentrated effort.

So, when did I shift to two-knuckles-typing and when did I notice? Whilst the answer to the later

361

occurred whilst in the midst of the rewrites of *Absolution in Neutral*, I have no answer to the former question. And why? Watching myself now, I would say a combination of laziness and comfort, though no explanation for the moment the change occurred. So now folks, I type with the second knuckle of my small finger on my left hand and with the first knuckle of the index finger of my right hand.

And I smile, recalling the disbelief of friends once I had dispensed with Bunny's typing services – *no way you typed that up yourself*. But I did and lo and behold, along came *virtually free* self-publishing … allowing the unpublished to publish … slashing the market and mark-up of the vanity press industry. I had been quoted £13,000 for the publishing of *Cannibals Eat Bods* back in 1988. My excuse for not biting that financial bullet was that I was not that vain. Indeed, you self con artist! Hasn't self-publishing actually allowed your vanity to run amok. Dear Reader, you decide. My defence would state that the fact that *Tacker Tomes* remains hidden from the publishing light of day says something … it says a lot, and perhaps its omission only goes to highlight my vanity.

As for no shame, well I am close to seventy (I repeat), I admit to sending out the *Absolution in Neutral* pack to potential literary agents with the knuckle typing as a novelty selling point. Hey, don't sigh in despair … this is the novelty world of TikTok. Gie's-a-break! Not enough of a novelty or the writing was crap or both; wrong place, wrong time. Whatever, I can hand on heart blithely state, for one thing's for sure, the rewrites of *Absolution in Neutral* greatly concentrated my mind during the winter of 2022 when stoma leaks could have so easily, nearly did, take me over the edge, even when the leaks occurred as my knuckles tapped out supplementary verbiage.

*

As my health continued to pick-up, I recommenced drinking pints at *Miss* Jones' Tuesday night pub soirées. Well knock me down with a feather but does David, a relative newbie, not pipe up with *you drink wine not pints*. Excuse me! All relative Nels, he has only seen the intermittent you, and then probably both pre and post reversal you were solely drinking wine after that one-pint experience.

Poor David, he means well (so we all say) but he seems to spend so much of his time bickering, a lot of it arising from being baited.

And I sadly realised that I can take or leave these Tuesday night bitch-fests.

I had not long shaken off eleven days of testing positive for COVID. I thought it was sheer tiredness I had felt upon reaching home from Simon's funeral. It was by some miles the longest round trip since stoma reversal layered with the emotional drain of the day.

Though I had had a couple of weeks to digest the fact that Simon was dead it was still somewhat hard to believe; the misdiagnosis; unbelievable stoicism, and rapidity. Then there was our last telephone conversation, I knew something was terribly wrong but had no idea who to advise of the fact. I tried to focus on the positive notes of our last meeting when he had been so up and happy about his hobby of trading at auction houses. Our private bubbles of harmless pleasure. What do us *single dots* amount to?

But I awoke the next day full of fever. It was COVID. Thank goodness for our vaccination programme, for other than two days of fever I was relatively fine … however ridiculous eleven positive days seemed. I duly isolated and the transformation of my bathroom into a wet room was put on hold, as my plumber's wife was expecting.

Personally speaking, the worst side effect of COVID was that my nighttime faecal bottom incontinence seemed to have a new and definitely unwelcome lease of life. Though by month end the dry nights had returned the resurfacing of such vigorous incontinence made me nervous about my pending nights away from home that were barely a month away.

October 2022

October 31st 2022
Output – 03:49 wind release with minor discharge.

Input – porridge and banana, daily medication, two mugs of tea, glass of clementine juice.
Output – 08:29 reasonably complete discharge though I feel some wind is still trapped.

Input – Aymes' vegetable soup (free sample from dietician), two

slices of white toast, easy peeler.
Output – 12:52

Thus, in mid-output concludes the *Dia-rears*, the title I glibly assigned to my food intake and anal discharge records of August through to October. I had been somewhat less flippant with my initial post-ileostomy equivalent; they were titled *Stoma Diaries*. But hey, the royal we was both older and wearier if not any the wiser. And my sanity needed amusement however scatological.

*

A random thought for October, I don't consider myself a spellcheck fascist but I must take issue with the car manufacturers. There now seems no end to the proliferation that started with Ford's Ka. Back in the good old days they had an Escort or Capri, and Leyland had a Marina or an Allegro. But now they are all at it. Ford has its Kuga, Renault its Captur. Need I go on. I want to. For I want to know how much Renault paid for the dropped *e*? Wouldn't you like to too? Would now typing *Desmond* [Tutu] be classed as flippance personified, as well as defeating the point, if there was one.

Some might say stop. STOP, you are now healed …

And as for the Vauxhall Mokka? Make mine an Americano with hot milk on the side.

STOP!!!!!!!!

*

Waste. And waist. They could be synonyms in and of my life. How perhaps, in fact most likely, my abhorrence, yes, it's that strong, of waste has affected my waist and, in the process, landed me in trouble … to the extent of my blue light experience of October 2021.

Growing-up waste was severely frowned upon to the point of intolerance, if you put it on your plate, you ate it. I thought leaving home would see a lessening of the strictures of home dining, but in fact the reverse occurred. And, I actually saw it become obsessive the more it was remarked upon. Simon and I were of a similar ilk, which did or didn't help, depending on how you looked at it. I know I would laugh it off with *it's the Scot in me*, always a grain of truth, as well as the fact that it was now my own dosh that I was forking-out and budgets were tight for quite some years. Food waste meant money waste.

Supermarkets are so adept at changing their product ranges, and you can psychologically convince yourself that it's your favourites that they keep ditching from their revolving product range. It seems to me from my various stop-start years of cooking for two or cooking for one that the range of products for one have been more plentiful in some years than others, across the supermarket spectrum, newcomers included.

Towards the end of the novel *Absolution in Neutral* Dave Claythorpe receives a letter from the council because he does not put out his food-waste bin. A man after my own heart, he has no food waste. Buy it consume it. Own it. Okay, no need to get carried away by today's jargon Mr Nearly Seventy!

But I know, and very stupid of me I also know, is that if I have cooked too much of something I will in the past force feed myself like a French pâté bound goose to the point of bursting rather than say the like of *okay, put that down to experience*. The whole stoma experience has made me refine my pre-cooking food measurements and I invariably no longer have seconds let alone thirds … the payment of the price now knowingly too high, regardless of discomfort, bloating and breathlessness. The later now looms so large in my life.

The need to expel wind so as to give my diaphragm more room to vent in and out. At times I burp with uncontrolled facility, awkward if at mealtimes in company, but better out than in for me. Nowadays, with regards to releasing wind from my anus, which I pre-stoma had a great facility with, this is a very fraught area of my life, for other than the sheer difficulty that I now have with expelling it the question of stick or twist, dry or wet. Can I risk relaxing my buttocks whilst out and about or do I need to be sitting on a toilet seat? Yes, there has over the past months been an improvement in this area, in that drier wind is dispensed than before but it's still not failproof. Poof, and you have wet yourself.

And the bottom line, again and again, is so much wind despite the fibre free diet.

November 2022

Off to Zambia I went. Who would have thought it. Hurrah!

All my precautions were unnecessary, but they put my mind at ease and perhaps that's why they proved to be unnecessary. For even though October had been a comparatively continent month viewed alongside the COVID hit month of September I was not convinced that this dry state of affairs was here to stay.

On safari holidays the internal small plane flights limited one to a total of fifteen kilos of luggage.

Despite having to travel light into my packing I squeezed in a disposable nappy for each of the twelve nights away, plus one for each of the overnight international flights. So dry were my nights that I returned home with eight of the nappies unused. As I know how fascinating this is I used one nappy three times at each camp, treating myself to a fresh one as we moved camp. Riveting stuff, eh? It was to me, and I have to admit that although wearing a man's diaper was somewhat reassuring it was not completely so ... the recall of the night before my potassium collapse was still a fresh mess in my mind. But having tried my friend Dr Begg's loperamide advice before my holiday I was more hopeful of being in control than I had been the week before. So, tell me, why were the medics not able to suggest this as the way to manage night time incontinence? Rhetorical! Though it shouldn't be ...

And I did use loperamide. On occasion, post-use I did wonder to myself, for I did not choose to divulge each morning over breakfast the contents or lack thereof of my nappy, whether I had taken them as a placebo. If this was the case it worked, yet I was also careful not to overdose as I did not want to be bunged up, especially not with trapped wind. The latter has been an Achilles' heel of my life.

I was surprised, delighted even, that my bottom continence was proving not to be an issue on the safari drives. This was just as well as squatting was not something that I could do, I had not been able to for years. Even back in 2008 I had had to use the walls of the hole in the floor at the Turmi campsite in Ethiopia … don't remind me. In fact, I barely needed any safari drive toilet breaks, and I was drinking water to keep hydrated forever checking that my urine remained on the lighter side of lemon-yellow.

The loperamide did come into its own at the last camp, Fig Tree in Kafue, at least until we managed to convince everyone that we did not require rich fine dining at every meal. The shock when I asked if I could have a poached egg on toast for lunch. Keeping it simple is good.

*

Bag changes retrospective?

Record breaker? On the 28th of March I had five stoma bag changes within a twenty-four-hour period. Extracting this information from a diary is interesting, reading it somewhat coldly in black and white after a modicum of white phlegm bottom discharge last night. My current angst as opposed to that of last spring. Yet a five bag-a-day event would have been soul destroying last March. A combination of the event itself as well as the layering effect of uncertainty, how will the stoma bags behave today? It certainly gives you a foresight into the psyche of the half-empty individuals, who do nothing but worry about *what if?*

Looking back as a means to keep going forward, recalling what it was like in the days when you did battle with your mind as well as your body.

And here you are, attending football again, when there isn't a November/December World Cup hiatus.

There's SE25 and NW8, there's Avenue Road and there's Avenue Road; the latter, apparently the most expensive street in London, with average house prices over one and a half million pounds, in SE25 the average comes in, as I type, at under a sixth of that figure.

The relevance if any is not that, rather it's the fact that I just cannot believe the lack of imagination … Avenue Road! Road Street, Avenue Way, Drive Lane … please town planners, brighten up the day. The Avenue Road sign stares at me once parked up for Palace's home games, and I wonder who won the naming rights.

And on that note, here ends this particular digression.

December 2022

I am entitled to fears. I am entitled to loath some thoughts that I cannot shake off. Entitlement. I am entitled.

Entitled.

And yet I still find room for mirth, be it flippant or from the pending gallows as to everyone's clamour for entitlement. I praised Sebastian Coe and his cohorts for how they placed the 2012 Paralympics and how the country embraced them and how, as a result, our national psyche was forever changed.

But the entitlement they released alongside ethnicity and sexual orientation has created a mushroom of a nuclear cloud.

Entitlement! The title part of the word always makes me feel that there is a sense of responsibility inexorably linked to it, but I also feel that I am in the minority with this view of the etymology. *Coz we're entitled like.*

So, basically my fears revolve around another blockage and waking up with another stoma and bag … returning to the hamster's wheel cycle. Or cycling completely off piste with my metaphors! My diet and food input are no longer carefree, a small price to pay … my nosher entitlement lost. The privilege of eat-all-you-want denied, now so wary of the cost of accepting a second helping or having an unnecessary dessert. Lacing the return-of-the-stoma fears is night time anal incontinence; actually, a harder judgement call and there has yet to be a pattern to what causes these random botty-leaks. I can manage extra loose bowels that verge on qualifying as diarrhoea with loperamide but it seems that I have no control over the impromptu whilst asleep discharge … so holidays and sleep-overs have an additional stress frisson that is quite uncalled for. Definitely not part of the entitled I signed up for …

The hardest part is that it is basically down to myself. After the excellent dietician visits during my C-diff confinement at the PRUH there followed, at my request from my doctor's surgery, a one-off visit from the dietician sourced from Bromley Healthcare Services. The only person to read any part of *Dia-rears*! However, the surgery decided not to follow through with her advice on how to build up my weight. End of. Unless I create, and there comes a point of battles to fight and wars to win and as she basically confirmed that my diet was sound onwards I go.[5]

I tend to eat sensibly at home, experimenting warily … my diet remaining what it has been

---

[5] Bromley Healthcare Services made an appointment for a follow-up telephone call a year later. I advised about my loss of weight, *disease-related malnutrition* their conclusion. Once again, by phone I was prescribed build-you-up drinks and soups. But this time I received written confirmation of their prescription. Three over Christmas visits to the pharmacy later, *sorry Mr Andrews, no prescription*. I phoned the surgery – the Healthcare's letter had been filed without being actioned. So, that's what happened in 2022!

since October 2021. As to my eating out, it depends if it is pre-theatre, then caution prevails, even though whatever I eat out inevitably causes loud enough tummy rumbles for my carer to hear above the on-stage performance. A concern for liking front row seating at the Hampstead Theatre. If I am out for a meal that will mean home afterwards, I might be more daring. Might! It depends on what has gone, or come out, in the recent past.

I am entitled to gasp for breath, wondering where the next one will come from as my diaphragm is compromised, that is squeezed into accordion-like submission by my captured wind … I was back in hospital at the beginning of the month. Against my better judgement I eventually made the right judgement and called an ambulance in the early hours of the Wednesday morning, confirmed to be the right call by the crew. I had pneumonia, much to the relief of Mary-Jane who caught sight of me on the Surgical Ambulatory Ward – now an actual ward with beds – at a more sociable hour later that morning. She was as relieved as I was that this hospital stay was nothing to do with the stoma reversal. But let's be honest about this, it's all linked back to my AMC and my diaphragm's being the constant victim of the stomach's bullying.

Fascinating, as long as not applied to you, to have two medical disciplines fight over cause and effect. I swallowed the flush-you-out laxative and duly fell asleep after two toilet trips and woke up to be transferred to go to the scanning theatre to discover that my bowels opened during the snooze, and thus there was the need to clean me up, however perfunctorily. The same happened once back in my bed as the last of the laxative did its best! Oh, the joy, recalling the summer's buttock clenching diarrhoea extravaganza. To top off this brief hospital sojourn I was physically moved out of my four-bed side ward to an isolation room … just in case the antibiotics I had been put on for the pneumonia triggered C-diff. And it was *the land of the forgotten* all over again, as I was having a rant at the nurse for the fact that I had not received any breakfast Mary-Jane was on her ward round, though strictly speaking I wasn't her patient. It seems that the *nil by mouth* of the previous occupant had not been amended. I wonder how long it had been since anyone had used this particular room, for it had the feel of being an ad hoc storage facility; fans, blood pressure machine stands. Mary-Jane decided my bluster indicated that I was well enough to be discharged. And, so I was from this room's confinement, even if somewhat trepidatious about returning home. Tony very kindly came over from Essex, took me home and got me settled back indoors. My breathing was definitely much better than a week before, when I had had the first indication of this current breathing issue as I walked up the gentle slope on my walk home from a Spanish omelette and chips lunch at the local café.

Home and fit enough for the wedding of Tony and Sue G's eldest. Yippee!

*

What was it about me and hospital stays that make me change into a completely different being? Okay, I was ill, very ill, very, very ill even … but as I recuperated, I found it nigh impossible to shake off this zombie like feeling, where all the volition I had outside of hospital life was dissipated. The only exception was the brief post-stoma op stay due to dehydration where I didn't feel at all ill, and where the general anaesthetic fug finally cleared. But the potassium/c-diff and pneumonia stays did not involve a general anaesthetic, but nearly all my hospital stays involved major sleep deprivation. Major! Even as I recovered the Neil Andrews bite after the initial stoma op, I was kept awake for long periods of the night courtesy of the geriatrics with dementia who slept during the day but lost that solace at night. These souls were allowed to remain comatose through the clockwork meal times by the day staff, food intake dependent on the timing of their family's visits. On three of my hospital stays within *Stoma in a Teacup* I was in the room adjoining the nurses' station – try sleeping with the night staff obviously acting as if a day at work but forgetting that it was nighttime for their patients and that sleep is one of the best forms of recuperation. Forget it. Even the times I was not posted to a bed so close to their hub we would have YouTube videos playing on mobile phones permeating our darkened side wards; or the sound of their laughter ringing through the corridors.

Whilst not wishing my narrative to be pigeonholed as racist it was of interest to witness other races at it. On a couple of occasions I was witness to the Filipino mafia making life hell for an Afro-Caribbean staff nurse, where the Filipino staff dictated their break times and the night duty staff nurse had to nurse more than manage as the management rug was pulled from under her. Is that racism on their part or poor man-mangement on hers and racism on mine? Such the minefield we have created for our psyches to deal with.

During this particular spell of hospitalisation, I was also witness to two young nurses who should have been dismissed on the spot for abuse of mobile phone use whilst allegedly working. One of the old boys with dementia would not keep his oxygen mask on so needed supervision all through his (and my) waking night. Although the staff had drawn the curtains around his bed to either dampen the noise or hide the brute force needed to manage his reluctance to be force fed oxygen, I could see the glow of the lad's phone screen forever in the palm of his hand. Should staff be allowed to have their mobile phones on during their working day or NIGHT? I would say not. Any emergency call to a staff member should come through the ward, like when I called the ward I was on for a top up of my water jug ... a real emergency!

Then there was the hospital bed itself, which I did not find at all comfortable, even when fit enough to be able to work the controls myself. It was impossible when requiring the staff to make you comfortable for their patience was already stretched, let alone be able to cope with *no too high, sorry, can you raise my head up*, or *the second pillow has slipped*. You ended up with an as good as it's going to get compromise that was actually no compromise at all but an abject submission.

That's actually what I found the hardest to understand about my hospitalised self. I was more inclined to fight the causes of my fellow inmates than my own. Partly, and extremely sadly, in fear of the weakness of one's bedridden position and dependence on care, whereas retribution against those I was fighting for was unlikely if vocalised by a third party. My convoluted thought processes deemed so. My final couple of days in hospital after the initial operation were spent assisting the elderly gentleman opposite me stay alive, though admittedly against his will, *let me die* his evensong that he reiterated all bloody night, and my visitors became his life savers when my call button was not responded to with enough alacrity. (Yes, I know it's an oxymoron, call button and alacrity of response … but remember I am Mr Forever Blue Sky.) Then there was elderly Rod with hearing issues to defend. Is it so difficult for the nurse in charge to ascertain from either the patient or the next of kin how the patient prefers to be addressed? To my mind this is such an easy win, for patients of all ages. Above Rod's head was the name Rodney and with no mention of his being hard of hearing. The staff decided that Rodney, Roddy and Rod were all interchangeable and quickly became aggrieved at his lack of response. Other than the various name calling Rod also had thick accents to cope with. From the bed opposite I so felt for him as the pronunciations rained down on him, what was taken as being uncooperative was actually a struggle to comprehend, even if the spoken question had been stated loudly enough. My final straw in Rod's case was when a doctor with a heavy accent, perhaps from eastern Europe, attempted to converse with him. Time is money and all that, even in our NHS, but why was she talking to him on her own ... should there not have been at least one other member of staff with her or a member of Rod's family, someone to advise her of the fact that he was hard of hearing which heavy accented English compounded when it came to comprehension. It was not lack of cooperation. In fact, could lack of cooperation not be laid at her door? At the subsequent visiting time I reported her behaviour to Rod's nephew, it transpired that upon describing her that she was a doctor the family had already had issues with. Upon seeing my stare as she left Rod's bedside, said doctor gave me an *I give up* shrug.

Is the hospital care we receive based on our age? With one hundred percent care given to the eighteen and under population? Is eighteen the apex, with a gradual tailing off from there on in? I have previously mentioned that AMC specific care definitely ends at eighteen, my personal experience is that from then on it is a battle. And, again from what I have witnessed during hospital stays is that as you step through each decade's door your perceived entitlement from the staff's perspective appears less. When I think how readily my initial *do not resuscitate* stance was accepted. Take the lines I have written in the paragraph above, and elsewhere within this tale. It seems to me that the care of the defenceless aged is not the same as that given to our youth. As should be, perhaps, with limited (and ill-used) resources, but it should not be allowed to become the norm … passed off with a shrug. Next!

Stoma in a teacup

*

During the writing of the second half of *Stoma in a Teacup* I was reading Robert Sapolsky's *Behave*. Difficult as it is for a layman with a science education that ceased at fourteen to grok it is a worthwhile read and made me think, some of these thoughts seeping into the lines of my book. Though the word hippocampus was one I had heard before I would not have been able to give you a context; others like amygdala, glucocorticoids and thalamus I was pretty sure were brand new additions to my flippant vocabulary. I particularly loved glucocorticoids, even though I had trouble saying it when I tried vocalising it out loud. And I fancied creating a Cypriot Adonis of a medic with the name Glucocorticoids to be my physician! (But I stuck with Euripides ...)

Flippancy aside *Behave* made me question the origin of my innate optimism considering the fact that I was blessed with a congenital disability and had decided that Jesus did not actually love me on my first day at school. But where in effect the only failure has been in my sexual relationships as opposed to platonic ones. The latter manifestly successful by the extent of my friendship network, ranging from tell-all (almost) friends to acquaintances that flit across the pages of this life of mine at varying but generally irregular intervals, as interests coincide as well as fade, as partners and children arrive conversely to the death of others within the elliptical sphere of the hula-hoop of my life.

*

The pizza man loosely courted me for four years, indulging in the occasional street corner or bus stop snog ... but he was a bi sex addict and it was not what I was looking for. However, oh yes. The dreaded HOWEVER! However, I started to see him with appropriate social distancing during the first COVID summer – garden drinks and then supper. Then I said *okay*, we could start seeing each other, and I never saw him again. All I received was a WhatsApp saying it wasn't me but that he had a lot going on. That has also been an almighty unanswered itch. But as advised, it is my scratching post not his, if there had been any consideration of the me then it would not have ended in mid-sentence as it seemed to do. Was the chase all there was? Pay-back for my years of prevaricating wariness? Does it matter? It shouldn't. Defining moments in that pizza man was to be the last man that I allowed myself any emotional attachment to. The proof's in the pudding and all that cliché claptrap that is in essence true. The four years of *get away with you* had been the wise ones, I had allowed the pandemic to cloud my judgement as well as indulge my fantasy and it must be said VANITY. How could a forty plus fancy this sixty plus, and a disabled one too? The trouble with me was that I liked him for reasons that were definitely not woke; straight-acting top of the list, then he liked football despite being a West Ham fan, and, we had both worked in The City. Perversely, the fact that he had a ready-made family, well his son seemed somewhat neutral towards him though his wife (still legally not his ex, so her financial reasoning went) had turned his older child against him. Even if she was totally (and understandably) affronted at finding out what her husband was doing with other men (and women) was she not abusing her position as a mother in the graphic information downloads their daughter was made privy too? See, despite it all I can take a considered view of pizza man's predicament. I know folks, I am generous to a fault. But let's not start counting my faults.

As good as I am at both keeping secrets and promises I can't stop reality being weirder than fiction. And how shallow am I to even think of that two-dimensional pizza man in the same breath as …

Now here's something that I haven't even shared with Karen. Are you holding your breaths? He shares everything with Karen. Not quite. Not at all. Definitely not all.

Anyway, after the disaster that was pizza man. (I keep wondering whether he is worthy of capital letters? On the whole he is not worthy of anything, so he shall remain small case. Such the extent of my retribution!) Anyways, what with COVID and that I had not really had that active a libido for an age, or so it seemed, or it was acting its age. Who knows? Who actually cares? Suddenly I felt a bit frisky, even at sixty-seven, and was trawling one of the gay dating (sex hook-up) sites and started chatting to a ginger hunk who allegedly was okay with my disability and guess what – we were going to meet and was I okay with bareback?

Now, do I divert my story here with how I came to possess two lots of PrEP medication? No!

Suffice it to say I did. PrEP medication's efficacy at preventing HIV infections has allowed barebacking to return without the Russian roulette gamble of my youth. It did tickle my fancy that PrEP is usually prescribed for those at a high risk of contracting HIV. What did that say? The undertone? Could I be a wannabe slut for an evening? I took the first PrEP capsule on the day I ended up being blue lighted to hospital and the rest is history. Coincidence? It had to be. My stomach had been building up to this crisis for weeks. Hadn't it? I have however, not taken one since, the need has not arisen, and yes, I would be most trepidatious too. However much the horn arises. Or in reality doesn't.

Actually, thinking on, I do feel the urge to divulge the tale behind my PrEP windfall. *Miss* Jones gave me one of his temporarily former lodger's supplies of PrEP when James, said temporarily former lodger disappeared back to the Republic, owing Bruno, another of *Miss* Jones's lodgers, six grand. With me so far? Just you wait! James resurfaces via WhatsApp with a cockamamie story about being incarcerated by his father for being homosexual. You definitely could not be openly gay in Roman Catholic Ireland ... to some, happiness on earth was still a sin, let alone being joyful and well, as for gay? So, James is incarcerated and then shipped across the water to Boston where he is locked up in a seminary for perverts that need re-educating on the ways of the sexual norm, if sex comes into it at all after the cold shower treatment. James does tell a good story. Let's be honest about this, all James's stories are good ones. Ninety-nine percent of the time James is also the star. Bruno is no longer Chris's lodger, but James once again is, and his stories are for sure blarney gold. Yet Bruno has allegedly received but one of the six thousand pounds back. OMG is James but an expensive escort or what?

Wind in the Wallows

Independent, I imagine would be my friends' choice as an alternative title to *Stoma in a Teacup.* Personally, I would now choose *Wind in the Wallows.* Perhaps with an accompanying expletive or two. Apologies. No. not for the expletives but for my cussed independence. As I sock and boot myself each morning, I think back to my despair of less than a year ago when this was beyond me. At first because of the stoma reversal and then because of the albumin inspired swellings, and how I am now able to count my blessings again. And by doing so wind everyone up even more with my blue sky take on life.

And I recall a carpark incident of a few years back. A woman came up to me with her *still time to go* parking ticket, I thanked her whilst advising her that I had a Blue Badge. *Lucky you*, popped out before she realised it. We both laughed. Yet I do look at the benefits. I used to say advantages, now that, even I have to admit, is a stupid thing. A Blue Badge is a benefit of disability to mitigate the disadvantage of disability. Better?

Am I a nicer person as a result of being disabled than I would have been otherwise? Hypothetical, agreed, but it is a thought that I often consider. And my equally as often conclusion is *yes*, for I know how much I temper down the pressure cooker of volatility. Who wants to be me?

*

Okay folks, there has to be an ending, a line in the sand, such a stupid expression, always makes me think of King Canute.

But there has to be an end, however inconclusive that is. I have survived? I am still alive over a year after the stoma reversal. And yes, though not perfect, the body is performing well enough for my quality of life to appear back to normal to most who peer in through the windows that have no net curtains.

I must say that there's a walking around in a haze sense, talking silently to myself, worried that a vocalised word might be picked up across the fence if my walk is outside. It's the time where I regret being single the most, fear of being boring and alienating those I count as close stops me opening myself up as readily as they seem able to do. I keep my own council, retain my fears dangerously locked up.

I say dangerously for I fear how I am becoming somewhat scared of making decisions … all sorts of decisions … from mundane food purchases to luxury holidays. Yes, that extreme a range. It also seems that in an attempt to slow down to keep healthy I fear a vacuum of inactivity that will do nothing but expand the extent of this ponderous deliberation benefitting neither my physical nor my mental welfare.

I know a large part of the problem is that along with my own health issues a lot of my more senior friends have either died or are in the process thereof with terminal illnesses. What were Ian Dury's reasons to be cheerful? Whatever they were they aren't mine. Exactly, his not mine. And the point of this rant is that I have allowed myself to be physically frozen by imaginary headlights that I seem disinclined to be able to vocalise to interested parties. Most especially Karen and Tony. Go figure! I know, from off guarded looks, that both think something other than health is up, but with the health issues having been so dramatic in themselves, hiding within a post-stoma, post-C-diff world is all too easy.

Live life to the full. Find the right balance. Simon, my former flatmate, died and I focused on my first jaunt abroad since March 2019, followed by my first solo one in February 2023.

Do you know, what it is really all about is finding out what I really want to do. Yes, at lots of levels I appear to make a lot of choices, but I would state that an awful lot of these are based on doing the perceived right thing, be it as basic as being here for Gizzy to going to a play that *you* wish to see. As opposed to paring myself down to a core of selfishness where each decision is made solely along the lines of is this what I want. Stating it even this way, would I prefer to do nothing rather than see *your* chosen play, do nothing away from home as opposed to be at home with Gizzy on my lap.

Have I become too conditioned in regard to consideration? Years and years later, how I behave with coupled friends, the happy-go-lucky tag-along eunuch. Available to accompany the left-single of either sex. Except I don't charge, and perhaps I have missed something there. I could have been that most unusual of escorts, available to either or all sexes. Let's get woke!

Is that it? Is this selling myself short as well as being very disingenuous to my friends.

It isn't it, but there is something in there. Something that has now surfaced, where I am questioning motivation. The why of doing something as opposed to something else or even nothing.

Some call it the power of being able to say no as opposed to okay instead of yes, when the okay actually signifies an unstated no. Doesn't it? I feel I have had a life full of the unstated no.

Enough.

Enough, he states *sotto voce*, so much so he barely hears himself.

It's a condition from a conditioning which I very retrospectively try to unravel chicken and egg like. No actually egg and chicken like. Yes, it is that difficult. Homosexual or AMC? Disabled or gay? Neither, some intrinsic nature of my very own ... amygdala and hippocampus and amygdala. Thalamus? Glucocorticoids?

(I so love the word GLUCOCORTCOIDS. Once your tongue has mastered the double *co* it makes such a lovely sound. Sounds like a favourite vegetable. Makes reading *Behave* almost worthwhile in itself. Yes ... that is a jest.? Robert Sapolsky's tome is worthy, be patient with yourself ... halfway and you've cracked it. Well, that's my experience. And that's enough of yet another flippant diversion.)

A flippant diversion which to be honest leads me no closer to either understanding my lack of a *no* backbone or to how at this late stage, i.e., seventy approaches at speed, start saying *no* now.

Practice for the latter? Could do. Have started to do, on the quiet ... see if anyone notices. I used to think that I was selfish in my time giving.

How I ignored the warnings, choosing to clutter my life with acquaintances who, let's be honest don't give a damn and all too easily spit out the empty husk they have sucked dry. I now realise that I blew the few chances that arose because of not wanting to let people down ... so commitment after commitment were met, with, in the meantime, the potential main man losing interest, actually stating as Oscar has that I am far too busy for a relationship with ONE person.

Is it too late to declutter? Is it too late to find HIM? Never say never etc., but it's intrinsic, and I was surprised, pleasantly, when my libido returned. For over a year I thought that was it, the horn gone forever. Yes, there was some relief, but sadness too ... but it was merely dormant.

Though said Oscar put it into words I realised during our relatively brief Tinder and WhatsApp exchanges that I was top-heavy in friendships. How strange that sounds and yet I could not see a space in my diary for at least two weeks ahead, and even then, it would be a tight squeeze. Yet, there was a light, a way ahead, for all summer of 2023 I had kept September free of theatre dates … in case I was able to find a last-minute African safari deal.

What am I like?

*

It's the fear. It just never goes away. I assume it's how a cancer patient feels when on remission. And right away I feel guilty for comparing myself to a cancer patient.

But this fear, my fear is having to have another stoma. I couldn't cope. I know how close to the brink *Stoma in a Teacup* has brought me, *STOMA – THE SEQUEL* would kill me.

Could I laugh?

Am I entitled? To laugh? To cry?

Every meal, every poo, every sleep – when? Is it like being on remission? Meant with no disrespect to my friends on remission, what am I like, feeling bad about the fact I feel bad when others are worse off. I suppose that will never change?

Merely part of my standard rhetoric. I don't even know if daytime bottom incontinence is likely or merely one of my self-given exaggerated nightmares, but I know the tightness of control I currently exert to retain the forces of the would-be poo-nami! What happens when I no longer have such sphincter control? Recalling my worst experience with diarrhoea, man-nappies would not be able to contain my incontinence. Housebound at best. Commode bound at worst. It would be like my C-diff stay at the PRUH, supper eaten whilst diarrhoea exits my body.

Then there's the under-siege diaphragm, it's squeezed, and squeezed again losing its rightful space. Rightful in a *normal* body, hey! it's AMC here. Its battleground reduced, a seemingly pointless fight, a losing one against my capacity to build and withhold wind. So, I can't breathe and have to once again be given the outer body experience of a stoma so as to allow my diaphragm to be squash-free and the rest of me stay alive. *Stayin' alive!* NO! I don't want to live forever, but I don't want to live in fear either. I want to be able to breathe, not have to keep catching my breath, not have to hide my struggle, to suddenly stand still for a step takes my breath away. But on the condition, it's without a stoma.

And if any of the less than professional members of the health worker fraternity, private as much as state, were to read this I am sure they would not wish to have to *care* for me again.

Too much to ask? Well, there's a huge plus too, I don't want my nearest and dearest looking at me knowing what's going on in my head, twenty-four-seven. It's bad enough internalising it …

Stoma in a teacup

THE END

Acknowledgements

First and foremost, thank you goes to Elizabeth Williams, without whom this would not have been written, and then rewritten.

Thank you to Valerie Heasman – encouragement personified.

Thank you to elightcreate.com for grasping what the cover should look like.

It remains a hard tale to tell, my mortality appearing closer with every rewrite.

Stoma in a teacup

https://arthrogryposis.co.uk/ is the go-to site if you are interested in finding more information on AMC.

Thank you to all the EXCELLENT hospital staff.

But how I wish the rest of you would leave the health service.

The NHS template needs an overhaul which our *first past the post* electoral system will not allow.

Oh! for a statesman!

406

Printed in Great Britain
by Amazon

46418823R00228